Préface

Cet ouvrage s'adresse à tous les étudiants de classes préparatoires scientifiques (1re et 2e années) qui se présentent aux concours comportant une épreuve de synthèse de documents en anglais (Centrale et e3a, à ce jour). Il a pour but de les y préparer. Il s'agit de leur donner des conseils pédagogiques et de les entraîner avec des exercices ponctuels et des sujets in extenso.

La première partie a pour but, a) d'une part, de définir ce qu'est une épreuve de synthèse et ce que sont les attentes des jurys ainsi que la façon de procéder et, b) d'autre part, de donner des outils et des exercices. Vous trouverez aussi des conseils pour aborder les divers types de documents qui peuvent être inclus dans un dossier de synthèse et les critères d'évaluation aux concours. Un certain nombre de faits de langue (même si cet ouvrage ne se veut pas un ouvrage grammatical ou lexical) et de points méthodologiques sont expliqués.

La deuxième partie est réservée à l'entraînement. Elle comporte les sujets de la première session (2012) avec ce type d'épreuve, ainsi que d'autres dossiers. Chaque « file » comporte un sujet, une étape préparatoire à la rédaction et une suggestion de corrigé. L'étape préparatoire se présente sous la forme d'un tableau des idées à retenir, ce qui doit permettre au préparationnaire de vérifier que sa sélection est pertinente. Il est bien entendu que le corrigé proposé n'est qu'une formulation possible parmi bien d'autres.

Bon courage !

Partie I

Méthode

Chapitre 1

L'épreuve de synthèse

I. Centrale

L'épreuve à Centrale « sera une épreuve de synthèse de documents d'une durée de *4 heures. Quelques documents en langue étrangère (au minimum trois*) seront proposés aux candidats qui devront en rédiger une synthèse, dans la langue étrangère choisie. Les documents proposés se rapporteront à *un thème commun* pouvant intéresser le citoyen du monde (questions politiques, sociales, environnementales, etc.). Aucune connaissance historique, politique ou sociologique spécialisée ne sera nécessaire pour comprendre ces documents. Une *lecture régulière de la presse non spécialisée* sera suffisante pour appréhender le thème abordé et les documents proposés.

La synthèse devra *faire apparaître les arguments clefs de chaque article et faire émerger les lignes de force sans introduire de biais*. Le but est de réaliser un *exposé objectif* des idées présentées par chaque document, de façon que le lecteur de la synthèse puisse se faire sa propre opinion du sujet, sans avoir à consulter les documents originaux. Les candidats ne devront donc en aucun cas introduire de commentaire personnel.

La forme de la synthèse est totalement libre. En particulier, il n'est pas demandé de respecter la structure des documents proposés, ni de citer les auteurs ou les ouvrages d'origine, sauf bien sûr si cela permet d'apporter un éclairage particulier au propos. Le jury considère toutefois qu'une bonne synthèse doit *commencer en introduisant la problématique retenue*. L'utilisation littérale d'extraits des documents proposés est à proscrire, si toutefois les candidats souhaitent citer un passage, ils doivent suivre pour cela les règles habituelles (par exemple, l'utilisation de guillemets).

Il est attendu du travail demandé qu'il *restitue les éléments clefs contenus dans les documents proposés et qu'il montre comment ceux-ci se complètent, se renforcent, s'opposent, etc. La confrontation des points de vue proposés* dans les différents documents est un élément essentiel de la synthèse. »

« Les candidats devront *donner un titre* à leur synthèse. Il est attendu de ce titre qu'il soit *informatif et précis*. En effet, son rôle n'est pas d'inciter le lecteur à lire le reste du document mais d'*indiquer le plus clairement possible le thème abordé*. »

http://www.concours-centrale-supelec.fr/CentraleSupelec/MultiY/LVecrit/

Le sujet commun aux filières MP, PC et PSI est distinct de celui de la filière TSI et requiert une maîtrise plus fine de la compréhension de la langue. Les documents proposés dans chaque sujet correspondent à la préparation suivie par les candidats en fonction de leur filière. La longueur de la synthèse demandée peut donc aussi être inférieure pour la filière TSI.

2. e3a

L'épreuve à e3a de langue vivante (3 h) est une « synthèse de documents (*2-3 documents*, articles, graphiques, etc.). C'est la rédaction, dans la langue choisie par le candidat, d'une synthèse de plusieurs documents. Il s'agira de *documents d'actualité* au sens large du terme (textes, images, statistiques...), reliés par *une thématique commune*. Les candidats ne seront pas invités à donner leur avis (*ni opinion, ni commentaire*) sur les documents, mais à les synthétiser en *environ 400 mots* dans une *langue aussi riche et claire* que possible, en *montrant les points de convergence ou de divergence émergeant de la confrontation de ces documents*. »

http://www.e3a.fr/spip.php?rubrique29

Chapitre 2

Aborder les différents types de document

I. Un article de presse

a. Analysing press articles

- **Step 1:** study the paratext

  Newspaper or magazine and maybe its usual political stand, date, title (eye-catching, puzzling, ordinary)

- **Step 2:** first reading

  "Listen to" the text so as to get the gist (central issue, key point/theme/argument/facts) and deduce whether it is a news report or an editorial or a column

- **Step 3:** further reading(s)
  - Underline the key pieces of information using a highlighter for instance but do not over-highlight! Dismiss examples, proper nouns (except if the person is well-known and mentioning him/her relevant), trivial remarks, digressions…
  - Sort out this treasure-trove of information using the following notions: facts, causes, (positive/negative) consequences, problems, solutions, goals, arguments for/against, (dis)agreement, opinions, supporters/opponents, implications for the future, comparison, opposition, victims/beneficiaries…

- **Step 4:** spot style, tone, bias

  Warning!! Do not interpret, do not add anything!

  The English-speaking press
  - The British quality press
    - *The Financial Times* – a business daily
    - *The Times* – owner: Rupert Murdoch; right-wing
    - *The Daily Telegraph* – right-wing, very conservative
    - *The Guardian* – left-wing
    - *The Independent* – fiercely independent
    - *The Economist* – weekly magazine; liberal, right-wing
  - The American press
    - *The New York Times* – somewhat pro-Democrat, well-educated readership

- *The International Herald Tribune* – the international version of *The New York Times*
- *The Washington Post* – liberal
- *USA Today* – nicknamed as "McPaper"
- *Time* – very American-like weekly magazine
- *Newsweek* – weekly magazine (60% text, 40% pictures)
- *US News & World Report* – conservative, pro-Republican

b. Exercising with an article – File 1, doc 1

- **Step 1**

  A left-wing British newspaper

  2008

  A witty headline

- **Step 2**

  A news report

  The Chinese and South African policies about/ban on plastic bags – why? how? do they work?

- **Step 3**

  Highlight the key information/words in the article (File1, doc1), then very briefly sum up each part of it.

Handling plastics

Adapted from *The Guardian*, February 2008

While **China**, a world emerging superpower, is facing more and more environmental hazards, the mere issue of plastic bags may seem irrelevant, but aesthetics is not the key point. When discarded, **plastic bags are a burden on waterways, sewers, and soil**.

So, as one of its new year's resolutions, **China** has pledged to put a stop to its 30bn-a-day habit, and to **ban** the use of free and flimsy plastic bags by introducing **charges**. As of June this year, plastic bags must be paid for, and they will be banned from all public transport, airports and scenic places. *China's policy/ban & charge & the problems caused by plastic bags (pollution) as the origin of them.*

The thing is, **plastic is terrific**. Why? Its **multiple possible uses, its durability, its being waterproof, practical and truly cheap** are among its appealing advantages. But these benefits can turn out to be **doubled-edged** as with the case in point of the sheer **persistence** of plastic bags. *Positive & negative sides of plastic.*

The thicker they are, the longer it takes plastic bags to break down – up to a millennium. Their burning leads to **toxic gases** being released while the **stagnant pools** they create are the ideal ground for **malaria** to thrive in mosquitoes; and should **animals** consume then, which they well might, that is a cause of **suffocation or indigestion**. *Many negative sides of plastic*

Better waste management in Europe than in the developing world makes the threat of plastic bags less material there. *European vs developing world handling of the problem.* China's situation is perhaps better reflected by experiences in African places. [...]

The United Nations Environment Programme (UNEP) reckons **the South African ban** to be effective *Example of South Africa's ban & its means* – South Africans used to consume some eight billion plastic bags on a yearly basis. **Below-30-micron-thick bags have been totally banned** as they can easily blow away and turn out to be hard to recycle. There is **less littering consequently** now. **A charge** is in place and if people do not comply with the ban, penalties are really tough: **fines and even prison sentences.**

Before regulation was introduced in South Africa, the cost of producing, delivering and distributing plastic bags was concealed in food prices, so even if **customers** did not want a bag, they **would pay for it**. **Now they can choose** to pay and have a bag or not to pay – and UNEP reports that consumers have therefore benefited from **lower food prices.** *South African past situation and money perks of the ban.*

Nonetheless, consumers are still more prone to choosing plastic bags than paper ones or boxes. It seems that we are **addicted**. *But addiction to plastic bags.* What remains to be seen is **whether China can get rid of the habit, or find a truly fantastic – and biodegradable – plastic bag**. *Two options: giving up or biodegradable bags*

- **Step 4**

Pretty factual though doubtful at the end about China's case whereas praising the South African policy

2. Un dessin humoristique

a. Analysing cartoons

- **Step 1:** rack your brains to recall relevant words and phrases
  a) about this particular cartoon
  b) about visual items and their locations (*in the foreground / middle ground / background; in the top/bottom left/right-hand corner; at the top/bottom; on the side/edge; on the right/left*)
- **Step 2:** study the cartoon very carefully as nothing is left to chance. Spot
  a) size (small, large, blown up, shrunk)
  b) labelling (what, what for)
  c) speech bubbles (who, what, what for)
  d) symbols (what, what for)
  e) zooming (hierarchy of the elements)
  f) facial expression
  g) angle (sloping up or down, straight on, from behind, front on, on top or below)
  h) tone (satirical, humorous, ironic, amusing…)

  www.vcestudyguides.com/guides/language-analysis/10-things-to-look-for-in-cartoons
- **Step 3:** contextualisation

  As the cartoon is attached to a file, it must draw upon a point raised by it.
  - Does it support or oppose a point?
  - Does it focus on the past, present or future?
  - Which aspect and/or person of the file does it relate to?
  - Does it give further information?
- **Step 4:** interpretation *(use modal auxiliaries to qualify it)*
  - The message
  - The cartoonist's stand

Useful phrases

to compare sth with sth
to focus on a particular subject / a specific aspect
to imply / infer / suggest sth
to be a widespread idea among people
to attempt / try to give insights into a situation
to explain the true significance of sth
to poke fun at / to ridicule / to exaggerate a fashionable / trendy idea
to accuse sb of sth
to blame sb for doing sth
to denounce
to criticise
to oppose
to aim at making people do sth
to embody
to harbour various meanings
to enhance, to magnify
to convey the idea that…

Vocabulary

Nouns	**Adjectives**
a cartoon	funny
a cartoonist	witty
a drawing	humorous
a caricature	satirical
a caption	sarcastic
a balloon	cruel
a target	exaggerated
a satire	
humour	
wit	

b. Exercising on a cartoon (File2)

- **Steps1a & 2**

The Obama couple – to the left – and David Cameron – to the right – in front of 10 Downing Street, the British PM's home.

Formal dress & suit, smiling, waving, talking

Dressed like a servant or lackey or hotel groom, nonplussed & unhappy, wide-eyed, burdened

Carrying heavy pieces of luggage

Labels – economic and military subjects concerning both countries' foreign policies

Speech bubbles: playing with adjectives → ironic + implicit reference to "special relationship"

Forefront vs slightly behind

Bigger vs smaller, taller vs shorter

→ inferiority vs superiority

- **Step 3**
  - Relates to the relationship between the 2 heads of state & also their countries, especially with regard to foreign policies. Cameron / GB is merely there to implement / carry (out) the American decisions
  - Supports the idea of non-similarity between the 2 as in *The Independent*
  - Qualifies the idea of military and economic cooperation from the speech and the joint paper

- **Step 4**

  An unbalanced relationship in favour of the USA which needs the UK's help – on the field. Poking fun at subservience of GB to the US

3. Un graphique, un tableau

a. Analysing graphs, tables, charts, figures

- **Step 1:** rack your brains to recall relevant words, phrases and grammatical points (comparison, verbal forms and tense-and-aspect uses, quantifiers, expressing figures and ratios) (see below)
- **Step 2:** study the graph to spot the most conspicuous elements – do not go into too many details
- **Step 3:** contextualisation

  As the graph/table... is attached to a file, it must draw upon a point raised by it.
  - Does it support or oppose a point?
  - Does is focus on the past, present or future?
  - Which aspect and/or person of the file does it relate to?
  - Does it give further information?

➡ **Vocabulary – see at the end of the chapter**

➡ **Grammar**

◆ ***Comparing***

- **Examples**

  The figures were higher in 1967 than in 1987 / two decades later.

  There are as many people in favour as against.

  The production is twice as high as it used to be earlier on.

  There are four times as many teleworkers as there were two years ago.

  Fewer and fewer respondents are convinced by that idea.

As times goes by, British people are less enthusiastic about…

The wealthier people are, the more water-consuming food they consume.

Most of the resources on Earth are finite but there is more water locked than directly available.

The younger people are, the more likely they are to be on social networks.

- **Rules**

- Égalité

  as + adjectif ou adverbe + as…

  as + adjectif + a/Ø + nom + as…

  the same… as…

  not as… as… (inégalité)

  as much + nom indénombrable + as

  as many + nom dénombrable + as

- supériorité et infériorité

  - comparatif de supériorité

    adjectif ou adverbe « court » (d'une syllabe ou de deux syllabes en –y, -er, -ow, -l) + er + than…

    more + adjectif ou adverbe « long » + than…

    exceptions : good ou well → better; bad → worse; far → further/farther

  - comparatif d'infériorité

    less + adjectif ou adverbe + than…

  - superlatif de supériorité:

    the + adjectif ou adverbe d'une syllabe ou de deux syllabes en –y + est

    the most + adjectif ou adverbe « long »

    exceptions : good ou well → the best; bad → the worst; far → the furthest/farthest

    NB : s'il n'y a que deux éléments, c'est la forme comparative qui est utilisée

  - x fois plus… que…

    twice / three, four… times as + adjectif ou adverbe ou much / many + as…

- cas particulier : late
  later = plus tard ; latest = dernier en date
  the latter ≠ the former (celui-ci, celui-là)
- comparatif des noms
  more + nom + than
  less + nom indénombrable singulier + than
  fewer + nom pluriel + than
- superlatif des noms
  the most + nom
  the least + nom indénombrable singulier
  the fewest + nom dénombrable pluriel
- comparatif progressif
  the + comparatif + sujet + verbe, the + comparatif

Tenses & aspects

Examples

For a few years, opponents have been losing ground.

Since WWII, more and more countries have become democratic.

In the 90s, they worked mostly in offices.

In the 20th century, they used to travel a lot by plane but now they increasingly turn to electronic devices.

En bref

L'aspect « perfect » (bilan), le prétérit (action passée, achevée, datée ou datable), le présent simple (vérité ou observation générale, habitudes), la forme progressive (commentaire sur un processus en déroulement ou description)

Quantifiers

La totalité : **both / the two; all/whole; each / every**

L'abondance : **plenty, a lot, much** + nom indénombrable ou participe passé, **many** + nom pluriel, **several** + nom pluriel

Une quantité ou un nombre suffisant : **enough**

Une certaine quantité, un certain nombre : **some**

Une quantité indifférente ou questionnée : **any**

Une petite quantité, un petit nombre : **a little** + nom indénombrable ou adjectif ou adverbe ou participe ; **a few** + nom pluriel

Une quantité insuffisante : **little** + nom indénombrable ou adjectif ou adverbe ou participe ; + **few** + nom pluriel

Une quantité nulle : **neither; no; none; not… any**

- **Expressing figures and ratios**

  Cardinal numbers: one, two, three…

  Definite figures: digit + dozen / hundred / thousand / million / billion + plural noun

  Indefinite figures: Ø + dozens / hundreds / thousands / millions / billions + of + plural noun

  Ordinal numbers: the + first, second, third, fourth, fifth…

  Ratios: one / two… + quarter / half / third / fifth… (+s)

b. Exercising with graphs – File 7 – the death penalty

Two Gallup poll charts on opinion in the United States

October 13, 2011

Are you in favor of the death penalty for a person convicted of murder?

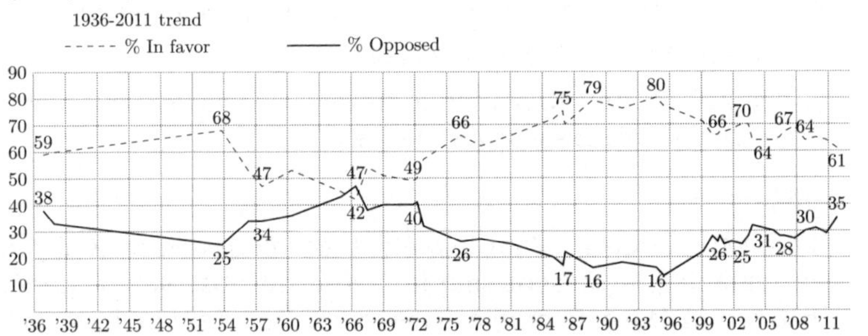

If you could choose between the following two approaches, which do you think is the better penalty for murder?

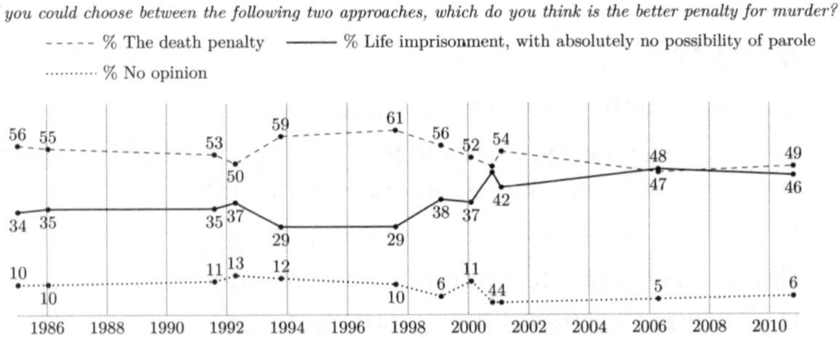

- **Step 1**

  Simple past, simple present, present perfect

  From… to…

  Almost as many… as… / on a par

  Slightly higher / more… than…

  Almost half of…

  One third… Three fifths…

- **Step 2**

  American people were and are mostly in favour of the death penalty for murderers with variations over the last 8 decades with a downward trend. But when given the choice between the death penalty and life imprisonment they have been getting quite evenly divided since 1986.

- **Step 3**

  Supporting the idea of the US as a stronghold of the death penalty though with a qualification (life imprisonment is getting more popular). Dwindling support for the death penalty even in the US.

4. Un extrait littéraire

a. Analysing literary excerpts

- **Step 1:** study the paratext (author, book, date of publication) and rack your brain for information you may know about it.
- **Step 2:** spot who, where, when, what, how
- **Step 3:** spot style, tone, literary devices, figures of speech
- **Step 4:** contextualisation

  As the excerpt is attached to a file, it must draw upon a point raised by it.

  - Does it support or oppose a point?
  - Does is focus on the past, present or future?

- Which aspect and/or person of the file does it relate to and/or illustrate?
- Does it give further information?

b. Exercising with a literary excerpt – File I – plastic

The Terrible Privacy of Maxwell Sim,
Jonathan Coe, 2010, ch. 9

[Trevor said,] "Alan saw what the majors were doing wrong. He saw where the future lies: green toothbrushes."

"Green?" I said, puzzled.

"I don't mean the colour, Max. We're talking about sustainable energy, renewable sources. Let me ask you – where do you think most toothbrushes are made?"

"China?"

"Correct. And what are they made of?"

"Plastic?"

"Right again. And what are the bristles made of?"

I could never answer questions like this. "I don't know… Something synthetic?"

"Exactly. Nylon, to be precise. Now what does that sound like to you? To me, it sounds like a recipe for environmental disaster. Dentists recommend that we change toothbrushes every three months. Four times a year. That means you're going to get through about three hundred toothbrushes in your lifetime. Worse than that, it means that in the UK alone, we probably throw away about two hundred million toothbrushes every year. Good for the big corporations, of course – it means people have to keep buying new ones. But that's old-style thinking, Max. You can't put sales ahead of the environment any more. For the sake of humanity, we've all got to change our tune. The profit motive has to play second fiddle. […] Now – Alan knew the solutions weren't difficult to find. […] Option number one […] a wooden toothbrush. […] Made from sustainable wood, of course – one hundred percent European pine. No damage to the rainforests here. And when you've finished with it, you can throw it on the fire, or shred it and put it in the compost."

[…] "What are the bristles made of?" I asked.

"Boar-hair," said Trevor.

- **Step 1**

  Recent novel, contemporary British novelist

- **Step 2**

  Who: narrator (Maxwell Sim), Trevor (character in the toothbrush business, for a company headed by "Alan")

  Where: the UK

  When: nowadays

  What: making environmentally-friendly toothbrushes made of wood and boar-hair, a green profitable innovation

- **Step 3**

  A naive narrator; salesman talk =) funny, comic

- **Step 4**

  raising the issues of throwaway items / waste, the environment, sustainability & especially plastic

  finding one solution to the problems entailed by plastic, an example

  + wider issue of protecting the environment (rainforests included) vs profit-making

5. Une publicité

a. Analysing an advertisement

- **Step 1:** rack your brains to recall relevant words and phrases
  a) about this particular advert
  b) about visual items and their locations (*in the foreground / middle ground / background; in the top/bottom left/right-hand corner; at the top/bottom; on the side/edge; on the right/left*) and advertising in general

- **Step 2:** study the advert very carefully as it is usually deftly contrived. Spot
  a) general impression at first glance (mood?)
  b) product or service or message promoted

c) how the components are arranged
d) the relationship between pictorial and written elements
e) symbols (what, what for)
f) use of space
g) facial expressions and figures (people, animals…)
h) background vs foreground
i) action, theme, plot (what)
j) type of language – information-providing or emotion-triggering?
k) Typefaces (what? what for?)

- **Step 3:** contextualisation

  As the advert is attached to a file, it must draw upon a point raised by it.

  - Does it support or oppose a point?
  - Does is focus on the past, present or future?
  - Which aspect and/or person of the file does it relate to?
  - Does it give further information?

- **Step 4:** interpretation *(use modal auxiliaries to qualify it)*

  The advertiser's message (What sociological, political, economic or cultural attitudes are indirectly reflected in the advertisement? Does it manage to strike a chord in consumers' needs and desires?) and goals (sell, promote, warn, make laugh…)

➡ **Vocabulary**

Nouns

advertising	a copy (= text)
an ad(vert)(isement)	visual elements
an advertiser	a logo
a picture	a slogan
a drawing	a target
a graph	a pun
a caption	a brand
a headline	a model
a sub-head	a lie

Verbs	**Adjectives**
to grab the reader	eye-catching
to catch the attention	text-heavy
to promote	persuasive, convincing
to sell	witty
to advertise	clever
to aim to do sth	commonplace
to imply	sexist
to identify with	dishonest

b. Exercising with an advertisement – File 1

If this ad had been part of file 1, how could it have been used?

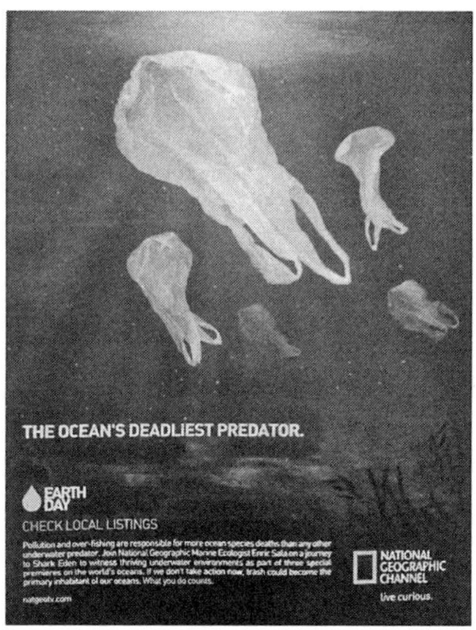

http: //www.sustainabilityconversations.com/2010/04/04/ad-of-the-day-17-plastic-shopping-bag-jellyfish-ads/

- **Step 1**

  Ocean, sea, marine life

  Plastic bags floating like jellyfish

  A threat; threatening; dangerous; jeopardised; in peril; pollution

- **Step 2**

  At first glance quiet and peaceful but misleading

  Goal: protecting ocean species from life-threatening discarded plastic bags. Earth Day, National Geographic channel. Getting people involved.

  The line in bold type / the headline prevents any misunderstanding and entices the viewer to look more carefully

  The text / copy explains in more details the goal of the advert. It is in small type but the last words ("what you do counts") are in bold colour type. The words used are emotional.

  The logo of Earth Day is a water drop to emphasise the message.

  A big plastic bag in the foreground catches the eye.

- **Step 3**

  Clearly this ad buttresses the arguments of the *Independent* article. Marine life is endangered by plastic bags which sea animals may be deceived by.

- **Step 4**

  The message conveyed is to make people react and act so that they do not dump plastic bags but join the efforts of National Geographic on Earth Day.

  A striking image.

6. Une photographie

a. Analysing photographs

- **Step 1:** rack your brains to recall relevant words and phrases
  a) about this particular photo
  b) about visual items and their locations (*in the foreground / middle ground / background; in the top/bottom left/right-hand corner; at the top/bottom; on the side/edge; on the right/left*) and photography in general

- **Step 2:** study the photo very carefully as nothing is left to chance. Spot
  a) size (small, large, blown up, shrunk)
  b) caption (who, what, what for, when…)
  c) symbols (what, what for)
  d) zooming (hierarchy of the elements)
  e) facial expression
  f) kind of shot (long shot, medium shot, close-up shot, lighting, colour, angle)

- **Step 3:** contextualisation

  As the photo is attached to a file, it must draw upon a point raised by it.
  - Does it support or oppose a point?
  - Does it focus on the past, present or future?
  - Which aspect and/or person of the file does it relate to?
  - Does it give further information?

- **Step 4:** interpretation *(use modal auxiliaries to qualify it)*

  The message

Vocabulary

Nouns

photography	depth of field
a photo(graph), a shot, a picture	a close-up
a photographer	the framing
the setting	the lighting
the layout	the focal point
a shadow	a high-angle shot
a reflection	a low-angle shot

Adjectives	Verbs
bright	to take a picture / a photo
pale	to centre
dull	to focus on
sharp	to highlight
blurred	to capture
artistic	
dynamic	
static	

b. Exercising with a photograph – File 6 – 9/11

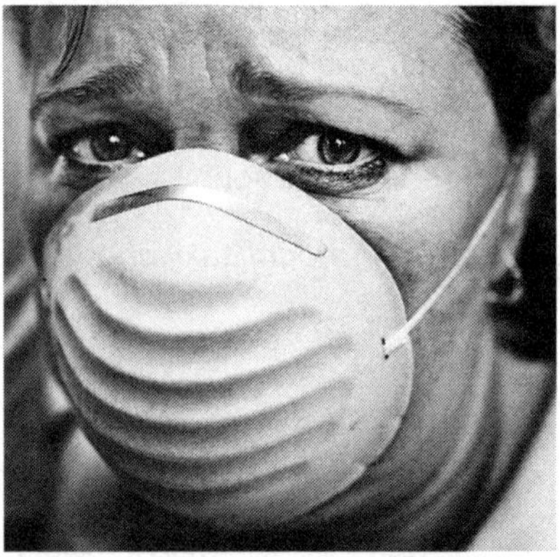

Mid-September 2001 (Photo: Peter Funch)

- **Step 1**

  A face

  Grief, sorrow, pain, sadness

  A dust breathing mask

  A woman (earring, make-up…)

- **Step 2**

  A blown up image; a close-up shot, not even the whole head can be seen.

  Focus on the mask and the eyes

  Stress and sorrow lines, on the verge of tears

- **Step 3**

  This photo is a vivid testimony of the grief of 9/11 victims' relatives and rescuers

- **Step 4**

  The photographer must have wished to capture a vivid striking picture for viewers to understand, sympathise and remember

Vocabulary: graphs, changes, evolution

Nouns

bar chart = histogramme
chart = tableau de statistiques
curve = courbe
decline = déclin, effondrement
deviation = écart
diagram = diagramme
digit = chiffre
downswing = baisse sensible
drop = chute
fall, decrease = baisse
figures = chiffres
flow chart = diagramme de circulation / d'acheminement
fluctuation = fluctuation
frequency = fréquence
graph = graphique
histogram = histogramme
index, pl. indices = indice(s)
jump = bond
measure = indicateur; mesure
number = nombre
pattern, trend, tendency = tendance
peak, summit = pic, sommet
percent = pour cent
percentage = pourcentage

pie chart = camembert
pyramid = pyramide
rate = taux
results = résultats
rise, increase = hausse
slope = pente, inclinaison
standard deviation = écart-type
statistics = statistiques
stratum = strate
table = tableau
trough = creux
upswing = hausse sensible
variable = variable
X-axis = abscisse
Y-axis = ordonnée
Z-chart = graphique en dents de scie
rank = rang, classement

- **Exercise:** sort out this vocabulary: type of visual element, going up, going down, high, low

◆ ***Verbs***

be level with = être au même niveau que
bottom out = atteindre un niveau plancher
bottom up = repartir après avoir atteint un plancher
check, curb, stem = freiner
collapse = s'effondrer
decrease = décroître
decline = décliner
drop = chuter
fall = chuter
fluctuate = fluctuer
go down = tomber, baisser
go up = monter, être en hausse

increase = accroître, augmenter

keep up / down = maintenir, contenir

keep / remain stable / steady = rester stable

level out / off = s'aplatir, s'aplanir

nosedive = piquer du nez, chuter

peak out = redescendre après avoir atteint un plafond

pick up = amorcer une reprise

plot or draw a graph = tracer, dessiner un graphique

plummet = tomber en chute libre, chuter très fortement, piquer du nez

plunge = plonger

raise = (faire) augmenter

rank first, second… = arriver en… position, se classer…

reach = atteindre

reach its lowest = atteindre son point le plus bas

reach its peak / its highest = atteindre son point culminant

rise = s'élever

see-saw = fluctuer en dents de scie

shoot up, soar = monter en flèche, faire en bond

skyrocket = grimper en flèche

slow down = ralentir

speed up = accélérer

stand at = se situer à

steady, stabilise = se stabiliser

top a figure / record = dépasser un chiffre / record

- **Exercise:** sort out these verbs: up, down or steady?

- ***adjectives & adverbs***

almost, nearly, close to = presque

appreciable, significant = sensible, significatif

approximately = approximativement

around = environ

broadly speaking = généralement parlant

cyclical(ly) = cyclique; de manière…
dramatic(ally) = spectaculaire; de manière spectaculaire
drastic(ally) = massif; de manière…
gently = modérément
gradual(ly) = graduel, progressif, doux; de manière…, peu à peu
greatly = beaucoup, considérablement et de manière positive
hardly, barely, scarcely = à peine
linear = linéaire
marginal(ly) = marginal
marked(ly) = prononcé; de manière…
qualitative = qualitatif
quantitative = quantitatif
quickly = rapidement
random = aléatoire
roughly = à peu près
seasonal(ly) = saisonnier; de manière…
sharp(ly) = fort; fortement, brutalement
slight(ly) = assez faible, léger; légèrement
slowly = lentement
steady(/ily) = régulier, constant; de manière régulière
steep(ly) = brutal; en flèche
substantial(ly) = sensible, significatif, substantiel; de manière…
sudden(ly) = soudain, brusque; soudainement, brusquement

Chapitre 3

Comment procéder

I. Méthode et gestion du temps

- **Lecture attentive :** ≈ 45 minutes sur 4 h, 30 minutes sur 3 h
  - nature des documents
  - paratexte (source, nationalité, date)
  - teneur générale

- **Thème et problématique :** i.e. question générale à laquelle chacun des documents répond à sa façon ≈ 15 minutes sur 4 h, 15 minutes sur 3 h

- **Tableau de confrontation / convergence :** ≈ 1 h 15 sur 4 h, 1 h sur 3 h

  Le premier document normalement est le texte-guide

  Une colonne par document : y reformuler les idées essentielles en faisant ressortir comment elles se rattachent à la problématique (cause, fait, conséquence, problème, solution, illustration, cas particulier, nuance…)

  Voir comment les idées de chaque document se complètent, se renforcent ou s'opposent d'une colonne à l'autre

- **Construction d'un plan :** ≈ 30 minutes sur 4 h, 15 minutes sur 3 h

  L'utilisation de couleurs (une par partie, sous-partie) peut être utile pour s'assurer de n'omettre aucune idée figurant dans le tableau

- **Rédaction et relecture :** ≈ 1 h 15 sur 4 h, 1 h sur 3 h
  - *Titre* : informatif et précis
  - *Introduction* : la problématique et une présentation rapide des documents (nature, origine, rattachement à la question)
  - *Développement* : 2 ou 3 parties maximum ; plan analytique (causes, conséquences, solutions ; faits, cause, conséquence) ou par catégories (lecture historique, politique, économique, philosophique, sociologique… ; sous-problèmes inhérents à la situation ; points de vue des différentes parties prenantes)
  - *Conclusion* : bilan objectif rapide
  - *Relecture* : corriger les erreurs de base (formes verbales qui existent, adjectifs invariables, accords en nombre, pronoms relatifs, ponctuation, déterminants, prépositions…) ; soin porté à la copie, nombre de mots, titre

2. Phraséologie

a. Introduction

The file is about / concerns / discusses, deals with / raises the issue of[1], and in particular / focuses on / centers on…

It includes / is composed of…

An (American / British / Australian…) (biased / objective…) article / a column / an editorial / a graph / a cartoon / an advert / a leaflet / a literary excerpt / a passage from…

An *Economist / New York Times / Guardian/…* article / column…

- **More useful / model sentences**

The article *was published in* (May) 2010.

The article *was published on* April 23rd 2011.

The editorial *is entitled* "plastic planet".

The article *is taken from* The Economist, a British magazine.

The article *was published in* The Times, a British daily newspaper / *on* the BBC website.

The book which is alluded to was published in 1976.

The main theme / subject / topic is…

The article *is focused on* the danger posed by…

The file *is about…*, a recurrent theme today, *and more precisely…*

It *deals with* capital punishment in the United States, *more specifically* about its implementation in Texas.

In the article, the journalist writes about the problems of…

The text deals with…, a highly controversial subject.

It is about…, a much debated issue in the US.

The file is about…, an issue which has become a political hot potato[2] and focused on by a 2010 *Independent* article, a 2008 *Guardian* column and a cartoon.

The article is based on a survey[3] of…, a survey carried out by[4]…

1. soulève le problème de
2. un sujet que les politiciens évitent
3. étude, enquête
4. réalisé par

- **Summing up**

  To begin with / As a starting point, what should be pointed out is the facts of this tendency.

  First, it's worth noting that...

  That therefore leads to consider the causes / consequences of this...

  In addition / What can be added here is that...

  However there are some solutions. Indeed...

  In a nutshell...

b. Sorting out and providing information

➠ The cause

The decision was made as a result of...

The incident was brought about[1] by...

There are several reasons for this... First... Secondly...

This crisis has arisen[2] due to...

The problem came to a head because of..., when...

The problem can be attributed to / is the product of..., an outgrowth of[3]..., stems from[4]...

➠ The central issue

The issue centres on the fact that...

The purpose of the talks / the experiment was to...

The crux of the issue[5] is that / lies in the fact that...

The main protagonists in the issue are...

➠ Examples

Several examples are given that illustrate / indicate / show that / epitomise / emphasise...

---

1. amené par
2. est apparu
3. le résultat de
4. provient de
5. point crucial, cœur du problème

First of all… Then… Lastly…

A few instances are mentioned that…

➡ The sequence of events

The problem first surfaced / emerged / came up / arose when it was discovered that…

A few weeks later…Then… At the same time… Finally…

➡ A debate

◆ *Criticism*

The proposal has been sharply criticised by…

There are, however, a number of critics[1] of the proposal

There has been a lot of criticism[2]

◆ *Arguments*

A debate has arisen concerning the project

The controversy is over whether or not…

The issue has stirred up[3] a controversy because…

This is a moot point[4] / a controversial issue because…

There are two main arguments in favour of / against / opposed to…

There are a number of pros and cons[5] on the issue

◆ *Positive and negative aspects of an argument*

There are several advantages to the programme… First…Then…

There are a number of disadvantages / drawbacks / downsides / dangers inherent in such a proposal

The plan has some positive features[6]… and some negative points…

The strong / weak points of the arguments are…

---

1. critique (personne)
2. critique (idée, opinion)
3. suscité
4. sujet à controverses
5. le pour et le contre
6. aspects

Agreement

X agrees with Y concerning

X is also in favour of Y's idea / supports Y's plan

Disagreement

There are conflicting opinions on the subject

X denounces the use of…

Contrary to / Unlike[1] X, Y believes, contends[2], claims[3], argues[4] that…

X considers it unwise, foolish[5] to…

X challenges the point of view of…

X objects to, disapproves of such a policy on the grounds that it could jeopardise[6]…

X questions[7] the right to…

X expresses misgivings[8] as to the wisdom of doing that…

Stating opinions

X says, feels, believes that…

X considers the idea to be irrelevant[9] to the problem at hand[10]

X views, judges, looks upon, regards the proposal as being irrelevant

Supporters[11] and opponents[12]

A majority of scientists advocate, support[13] an ethical view

Only a minority oppose, are against…

Advocates, proponents[14] of the policy claim that…

Opponents, adversaries argue that…

---

1. à la différence de
2. soutient que
3. prétend que, affirme haut et fort que
4. soutient que
5. imprudent
6. compromettre
7. remet en cause
8. doutes
9. non pertinent
10. problème présent
11. partisan
12. opposant
13. sont pour
14. partisans

Points of view and proposals

From the point of view of… the government should…

His objection lies in a reluctance to[1] take a stand[2] on a sensitive issue[3].

The proposal would involve, entail[4], necessitate…

X urged[5], encouraged, advised Y to…

Consequences

Such a behaviour may bring about, give rise to, trigger[6], lead to, promote, further, foster[7], create, contribute to, open the door to…

The outcome[8] might be to…

Beneficial effects

It will probably have a beneficial effect on the image of…

How can people be sure that… has really improved thanks to the new measures?

This trend favours, fosters, furthers the cause of…

His image was enhanced[9] and burnished[10] by his stand[11] on…

The breakthrough[12] is bound to[13] have a positive effect on…

… has been proved safe / harmless[14], reliable[15] and it has no harmful side-effects[16].

Thanks to… it is thriving / flourishing[17]…

Most people have everything to gain by it.

---

1. répugnance à
2. prendre position
3. question sensible
4. Impliquer, entraîner
5. conseilla vivement
6. déclencher
7. encourager, favoriser [qch]
8. résultat
9. agrandie, améliorée
10. dorée, redorée
11. prise de position
12. percée
13. va logiquement et sûrement
14. Inoffensif, sans danger
15. fiable
16. effets secondaires
17. prospère

Detrimental effects

It can be detrimental / damaging to…

It can only accentuate / widen the gap[1] between…

… has been proved unsafe[2] / dangerous / noxious[3] / harmful, unreliable[4]…

The measure may hinder[5] / get in the way of / undermine[6] / hamper[7] / endanger / jeopardise[8] / threaten[9]…

If a crisis is to be avoided, people have to learn from…

If people do not wish to undergo[10] another crisis…

The loss of… is one of the undesirable effects of…

Doubts and misgivings

There is overall agreement on the project. Yet, there are also reservations.

X expressed doubts on the feasibility[11] of doing so.

To some extent, X considers it worthwhile[12], but the cost is prohibitive.

Significance

The significance of this decision lies in the fact that it is representative / characteristic / symbolic / symptomatic of the current tendency[13] towards thinking in terms of…

---

1. agrandir le fossé
2. dangereux
3. nocif
4. peu sûr, non fiable
5. faire obstacle à
6. saper, nuire à
7. gêner
8. mettre en danger
9. menacer
10. subir, traverser
11. possibilité de réaliser
12. valable
13. tendance actuelle

This is a striking[1] / dramatic / appalling[2] / terrific[3] / unusual / typical / outstanding[4] example of today's preoccupation with…

It sheds light on…

➡ Patterns of trend

A sharp[5], steady[6] rise[7] **in** the number of people who…

A noticeable decrease / drop[8] in the number of…

A growing / increasing / rising, widespread[9] tendency towards…

People are increasingly / more and more prone to[10] / inclined to / likely to[11]…

They tend to[12]…

◆ **Present time** (*mind: simple present or progressive present or present perfect!!!*)

◆ **Past time** (*mind: preterit, past perfect, present perfect!!!!*)

➡ Root causes

Due to / Owing to / Because of / Thanks to… The roots of the problem are better known

This is only a symptom of a more serious problem. The underlying / root / deep / fundamental causes could be…

---

1. frappant
2. choquant, effroyable
3. super
4. remarquable
5. nette
6. constante
7. hausse, augmentation
8. baisse
9. répandue
10. enclins à
11. susceptibles de
12. ont tendance à

➡ Implications for the future

For the time being[1], the consequences of these findings[2] can only be guessed[3] at / surmised[4].

It may give rise to / bring about / foster / lead to / trigger / encourage…

The effects may be felt more strongly in…

The impact is likely to be far-reaching[5], extensive, limited to, confined to…

It is difficult to foresee / forecast[6], determine in advance the impact of…

It is hard to guess what the final outcome of… will be.

➡ Comparison and contrast

The situation of… in the *Economist* column can be compared to that of… in the *Guardian* article.

An analogy can be drawn between… and…

A comparison can be made between… and…

There is quite a marked contrast between yesterday's notion of… and today's.

The British approach to… differs from that in France to some extent. Indeed…

Nowadays… are hardly[7] different from one country to another.

There is hardly any difference between…

➡ Who feels the effect of the decision, event…

It's the poor people who will suffer most from that if…

Small farmers are likely to be hit the hardest.

This has had repercussions on all branches of the economy.

---

1. pour l'instant
2. découvertes, résultats
3. devinées
4. supposées
5. étendu
6. prévoir
7. guère, à peine

Editorial opinion

News reports

The article seems fair / impartial / unbiased / objective in that…

The journalist bases her / his opinion on the fact that…

The account / coverage[1] of the event seems biased in favour of / against…

It is partial to…

The reporter doesn't mention / leaves out the fact that… while the reviewer…

The report plays up[2] / plays down[3] / misrepresents / exaggerates / distorts[4] the positive / negative sides of the question

The journalists paints a rather bleak[5] / rosy[6] / depressing[7] picture of…

The report expects the outcome of the talks to be mostly positive while…

Editorials

The journalist points out that…

The columnist / newspaper may be right-wing, left-wing, liberal, conservative, moderate, reactionary as…

The journalist may speak for / defend / take a stand on behalf of…

Content, outlook, style

The journalist comments on the fact that… and remarks that…

The reporter suggests / implies / infers[8] / foresees that

The columnist urges[9] / recommends / criticises / voices concern about…

---

1. reportage, compte-rendu
2. Insiste sur
3. minimise
4. déforme
5. sombre
6. idyllique
7. déprimante
8. laisse entendre
9. conseille vivement

The style is humorous, witty[1], light, ironic, serious, dramatic since…

The text seems pessimistic / optimistic / convincing / unconvincing as…

The headline is eye-catching and actually harbours[2] a pun / a play-on-words[3] that contains the gist[4] of the text. Indeed it can be understood as… and as…

- ***The writer / cartoonist / columnist / photographer…'s intentions***

According to the journalist…

He states[5] that… He maintains[6] that… He asserts[7] that…

The journalist's purpose is to make readers aware of…

What the writer means is that…

His / Her intention is obviously to…

He / She tackles the problem of…, which is a growing cause for concern.

He / She weighs up the pros and cons of…

He / She analyses the advantages and drawbacks of…

This leading article is a scathing[8] attack on the proponents of…

He / She makes it quite clear from the start that…

He also alludes to another important event, namely[9]…

He takes several examples to prove his point[10].

He wants to draw the readers' attention to something that is essential.

He compares the two solutions suggested.

The message he's trying to get across / convey[11] is that…

1. spirituel
2. abrite, cache
3. jeu de mots
4. l'essentiel
5. déclare
6. soutient
7. affirme
8. virulente
9. à savoir
10. pour prouver ce qu'il avance
11. faire passer

The article brings home to[1] readers the pointlessness[2] of such a decision.

What he's trying to do is to shame readers into acting[3].

c. Utiliser des adverbes

actually = en fait
additionally = de plus
admittedly = il faut en convenir, certes
approximately, about, roughly = à peu près, environ
assuredly, certainly, undoubtedly = sans aucun doute
barely, scarcely, hardly = à peine
basically = grosso modo
conversely = à l'inverse
definitely = certainement, assurément
deliberately = sciemment, de manière délibérée
especially, particularly = en particulier
eventually, finally = finalement
evidently = de manière manifeste
formerly = autrefois
generally speaking = dans l'ensemble
gradually = petit à petit
incidentally = au fait, à propos
increasingly = de plus en plus
namely = c'est-à-dire
obviously = évidemment
oddly, strangely = bizarrement
possibly = éventuellement
presumably = apparemment
rarely, seldom = rarement
recently = dernièrement

1. fait bien comprendre à
2. inutilité
3. culpabiliser pour faire réagir

repeatedly = à plusieurs reprises
shortly = sous peu, dans peu de temps
similarly, likewise = de la même façon
simultaneously = simultanément, en même temps
slightly = légèrement
surely = sûrement
unexpectedly = de manière inattendue, à l'improviste

3. Exercices

a. Practice: sort out the information

➠ File I – plastic

Sort out the information from the file using the following categories: advantages, downsides, solutions + people involved, example of plastic item

- **Solution:** see "tableau de synthèse" ("steady")

➠ File 3 – space

Sort out the information from the file using the following categories: issue, consequences, qualifications, reactions, solutions

- **Solution:** see "tableau de synthèse" ("steady")

➠ File 4

Sort out the information from the file using the following categories: facts, partners, risks/obstacles/opposition, goals

- **Solution:** see "tableau de synthèse" ("steady")

➡ **File 8 – e3a2012 – tuition fees**

Sort out the information from the file using the following categories: facts/actors, risks/consequences/blames/concerns, reactions, recommendations

- **Solution:** see "tableau de synthèse" ("steady" dans la partie II)

b. Exercises to be more concise – compounding, word-building, and so on

➡ **I. Re-phrase the following bits to be more concise.**

1) networks that were used with a criminal purpose
2) as a consequence
3) the riots of August 2011
4) put the emphasis on
5) advocates of free speech
6) the users of social networks
7) the censorship of the internet
8) a murder committed in cold blood
9) an area devastated by a flood
10) mountains covered in snow
11) a man with an eager face
12) an area stricken by poverty
13) a woman with a kind heart
14) a period of mourning lasting three years
15) clothes stained by blood
16) an examination that racks nerves
17) a book which provokes thoughts
18) a package which was wrapped in plastic
19) a contract which lasts six years
20) a surprise which takes your breath away
21) a family which is dominated by males
22) a pump which produces water
23) a person with a bad temper

24) an event the aim of which is to raise funds
25) a situation which breaks your heart
26) companies which are owned by the state
27) a force which is meant to keep the peace
28) a decline occurring in the long term
29) the fact of knocking on doors
30) the people who do not vote
31) the people who are paid the most
32) a life of work having developed over 40 years
33) missions during which death is defied
34) a spike in the prices of oil in the 1970s
35) the drilling of oil in deep waters
36) a party which leans to the right
37) people who earn wages and are middle-class
38) that cuts benefits
39) that raises taxes
40) the minister in charge of the treasury
41) the system of social security
42) aid to navigate
43) barriers that are imposed by the state
44) a scheme that is sponsored by companies
45) factors that depend on cultures
46) targets that aim at cutting emissions
47) targets that aim at more efficiency in the use of energy
48) investments that aim at reducing emissions
49) events that change lives
50) in a peaceful way
51) for financial purposes
52) on an international scale
53) more and more
54) biodiesels that are brewed at home
55) biodiesels that are based on algea
56) manufacturing that does not entail taxes

57) a system that permits to deliver fuel
58) fat with a lot of calories
59) a system that gives a permit to work and which is sponsored by employers
60) the Arab League which includes 22 countries
61) its partner for trading which ranks second among its partners
62) a dictatorship in Libya which lasted 42 years
63) a regime which is backed by the army
64) a summit to discuss climate change and which takes place during two weeks
65) emissions of greenhouse gases in the whole world

II. Basis: File 6 – Try to rephrase more concisely the following sentences.

a) Franck Rich wrote an article for the *New York Magazine*. In his article he indicts Bush. There are also photos.
b) The photo which was taken in September 2001 shows the horror and grief that 9/11 entailed. The books of fiction that were mentioned earlier on do the same.
c) a memorial that is too obviously full of peace
d) Foer shows that memories can be very enduring and embedded in the minds of people
e) feelings against Muslim people
f) he blamed Bush because the President had implemented disastrous policies in the economic and foreign fields. Those were selfish and he had not thought them through well.
g) which put the US even more in debt and also entailed other terrible casualties
h) the greed of the Americans was caused by politicians

III. Based on File 4 – Try to rephrase more concisely the following sentences.

a) The file focuses on these suggestions. It is composed of an article taken from *The New York Times* which was published in 2010, an article taken from *The Economist* in an issue published in 2009, a cartoon which deals with obesity in the USA, and for the UK a webpage which was downloaded from the *Skynews* website in 2011 and an excerpt from the novel written by J.K. Rowling and entitled *Harry Potter*.

b) measures which are meant to fight obesity and which are related to food

c) to raise their awareness with messages. These messages are to be recorded by athletes. And media which are popular will broadcast these messages

d) to put labels on their menus. The labels will mention the number of calories

e) in the same way

f) proof that the government wants to act prominently and impinge on people's lives

Solutions

exercise I

1) criminally-intending networks
2) consequently
3) the August 2011 riots
4) emphasise
5) free speech advocates
6) social network users
7) internet censorship
8) cold-blooded murder
9) a flood-devastated area
10) snow-covered mountains
11) an eager-faced man
12) a poverty-stricken area
13) a kind-hearted woman
14) a three-year mourning period
15) blood-stained clothes
16) a nerve-racking examination
17) a thought-provoking book

18) a plastic-wrapped package
19) a six-year contract
20) a breath-taking surprise
21) a male-dominated family
22) a water-producing pump
23) a bad-tempered person
24) a fund-raising event
25) a heart-breaking situation
26) state-owned companies
27) a peace-keeping force
28) a long-term decline
29) door-knocking
30) non-voters
31) the highest-paid people
32) a 40-year working life
33) death-defying missions
34) the 1970s' oil-price spike
35) deep-water oil-drilling
36) a right-wing party, a right-leaning party
37) middle-class wage-earners
38) benefit-cutting
39) tax-raising
40) the treasury minister
41) social security
42) navigational aid
43) state-imposed barriers
44) a company-sponsored scheme
45) culturally-dependent factors / cultural factors
46) emission-cutting targets
47) more efficient energy-use targets
48) emission-reducing investments
49) life-changing events
50) peacefully

51) financially
52) internationally
53) increasingly
54) home-brewed biodiesels
55) algae-based biodiesels
56) tax-free manufacturing
57) a fuel-delivering system
58) calorie-rich fat
59) an employer-sponsored work-permit system
60) the 22-country-strong Arab League
61) its second-ranking partner
62) the 42-year-long Libyan dictatorship
63) an army-backed regime
64) a two-week-long climate-change meeting
65) worldwide greenhouse-gas emissions

exercise II – File 6

Here are the matching bits from the correction suggested

a) Franck Rich's *New York Magazine* Bush-indicting article and accompanying photos
b) The September 2001 photo bears witness as to the horror and grief entailed by 9/11; and so do the books of fiction afore-mentioned
c) an all-too-obviously peaceful memorial
d) Foer shows how enduring and mind-embedded memories can be
e) anti-Muslim feelings
f) blaming Bush for his disastrous ill-thought-out and selfish economic and foreign policies
g) further indebting the US while entailing further terrible casualties
h) politically-engineered American greed

- **exercise *III* – *File 4***

Here are the matching bits from the correction suggested

a) These suggestions are the focus of a 2010 *New York Times* article, a 2009 *Economist* article and a cartoon dealing with US obesity and a 2011 *Skynews* webpage and an excerpt from J.K.Rowling's *Harry Potter* for the UK.

b) food-related anti-obesity measures

c) to raise their awareness with messages recorded by athletes and broadcast by leading media

d) to calorie-label their menus

f) Likewise

g) proof of impinging big government's action

Chapitre 4

Les critères

I. Richesse et correction grammaticale

Toute faute rendant la synthèse inintelligible est à proscrire. Au bas mot, les structures élémentaires doivent être maîtrisées et le tout doit être compréhensible même si ce n'est qu'au moyen de phrases courtes et simples. Bref, grammaire et syntaxe doivent être correctes.

Sont bonifiés les structures et temps complexes utilisés à bon escient et correctement, la richesse et la variété des structures grammaticales, verbales et syntaxiques et, crème de la crème, une remarquable maîtrise grammaticale telle que celle d'un anglophone instruit.

a. Correction grammaticale

Toutes sortes d'erreurs sont possibles. Les plus fréquentes relèvent des accords en nombre, de l'emploi des temps, des constructions verbales, des auxiliaires modaux, des articles, des quantifieurs, des pronoms relatifs, des prépositions, de l'ordre des mots, des structures avec enchaînement de deux verbes, et de la ponctuation.

Bien souvent ces erreurs sont commises par inattention. Pour les éviter, il est souhaitable de se constituer **une check-list des erreurs** que l'on commet fréquemment de manière à les corriger lors de l'écriture et/ou de la relecture de sa copie. Cette liste se constitue préférablement devoir après devoir au cours des années de préparation.

Il existe quelques principes de base en anglais quant à **l'ordre des mots** :

- un adjectif épithète est toujours placé devant le nom qu'il qualifie ;
- un adjectif numéral vient tout de suite devant le nom qu'il quantifie ;
- le sujet est toujours placé devant le verbe sauf dans les phrases interrogatives ou les propositions commençant par une négation ;
- les compléments circonstanciels viennent en début ou en fin de phrase et ne séparent donc pas le sujet du verbe et le verbe du complément d'objet ;
- les adverbes de fréquence sont placés devant le verbe (sauf « be ») ou après le premier auxiliaire dans le cas d'une forme verbale composée ;
- l'ordre des mots avec « such », « quite », « too » et dans les propositions négatives doit aussi être connu ;

– enfin, alors que « also » se place devant le verbe, « too » vient à la fin de la proposition.

La **structure d'une phrase** est fondamentale puisqu'elle dénote la maîtrise de l'expression et de la pensée. Ponctuation et mots de liaison (voir plus bas) en sont des éléments essentiels. Au minimum, une phrase doit comporter un sujet, un verbe et un complément. Les phrases nominales sont rares et essentiellement de type journalistique en anglais. Il faut éviter les phrases trop longues et alambiquées qui noient le lecteur. Mais des propositions subordonnées (notamment relatives) construites avec pertinence permettent de souligner la cohérence logique des éléments mis en relation. Attention à ne pas attribuer un double sujet à un verbe en calquant la tournure présentative du français « X, c'est Y » (en anglais, « X is Y »).

La ponctuation utilisée à bon escient doit permettre d'écrire des phrases ni trop courtes, ni trop longues. La virgule est moins fréquente en anglais qu'en français. En particulier, on ne met pas de virgule après « but », « yet », « and », « so » ou « that's why ». Pas de virgule non plus après un complément circonstanciel donné en début de phrase. Il faut aussi distinguer le pronom relatif « which » introduisant une proposition à but de définition (pas de virgule) et le « which » qui doit être précédé d'une virgule s'il reprend ce qui vient d'être dit ou si la proposition (descriptive) qu'il introduit est un ajout d'information. Il est bon de penser à utiliser des points-virgules (pour montrer un lien entre les deux idées avancées) ou deux points (pour donner une explication ou clarifier les choses) à la place d'une virgule. Enfin, les tirets sont plus fréquents en anglais qu'en français : ils peuvent remplacer des parenthèses, un point-virgule ou deux-points.

Les mots de liaison (conjonctions de coordination, conjonctions de subordination, prépositions, adverbes) doivent être employés pour souligner les liens logiques entre phrases, propositions ou groupes de mots au sein d'une phrase ; mais il ne faut pas non plus en abuser. Penser plutôt à un mot bien sélectionné par paragraphe qu'un mot par phrase sans vraie pertinence. Quand le lien est clair, nul besoin de l'exprimer. Prendre garde aux emplois distincts de « though », « contrary » et à la confusion entre « despite » suivi d'un groupe nominal et « although » suivi d'une proposition subordonnée.

NB : Vous pouvez vous préparer en relevant les mots de liaison utilisés dans les corrigés proposés (« go » dans la partie II)

b. L'authenticité idiomatique (grammaticale et lexicale) à l'écrit

Il ne s'agit pas de l'anglais parlé oralisé, ni de l'emploi du franglais (mots anglais utilisés en français mais au sens souvent différent), ni d'un anglais ultra formel et pédant, ni d'un anglais scolaire (avec l'emploi artificiel de tournures toutes faites), ni d'une prose anglaise pseudo-littéraire (les expressions, proverbes, etc. ne sont appropriés que dans un contexte particulier que seule une pratique longue et assidue de la langue permet de maîtriser).

Certaines tournures et mots dénotent un calque sur le français comme « numerous » pour « many », « there is / are X which does… » pour « X does… », « it is X who said » pour « X said… », « reproach » pour « blame », « reductions » for « cuts », « phenomenon » pour « fact / situation », « project » pour « plan », « reduce » pour « curb », « forbid » pour « ban », « evaluate » pour « assess », « evolve » pour « change », « increase » pour « rise / soar » ou encore « decrease » pour « drop / plummet ».

De manière générale, il est préférable d'employer a) des mots d'origine anglo-saxonne plutôt que latine, b) des mots courts plutôt que des mots longs, c) des verbes, adverbes et adjectifs plutôt que des noms, d) des verbes à particule plutôt que des verbes simples, e) le passif qui est très courant en anglais (notamment dans la correspondance au « on » impersonnel du français), et f) des auxiliaires modaux plutôt que des adverbes ou des tournures impersonnelles. Il faut avoir à l'esprit que l'anglais est une langue plus concise que le français (pensez aux tournures causatives, résultatives ou encore aux verbes de mouvements suivis d'une préposition de déplacement).

2. Étendue et précision lexicale

Un bagage lexical indigent rendant le discours incompréhensible est à proscrire. Il faut un minimum de variété et d'authenticité dans le choix des mots. Ce choix doit être pertinent. Les mots français ou calqués sur le français « au petit bonheur la chance » sont une hérésie. L'orthographe des mots doit aussi faire l'objet d'une écriture et d'une relecture attentives.

Le registre doit également être pris en compte et correspondre à un exercice écrit officiel.

Les imprécisions et paraphrases pour éviter les répétitions sont tolérées, mais sont bonifiées la variété et la richesse lexicale dénotant la maîtrise d'une langue riche, appropriée, nuancée et idiomatique.

Juste est le mot qui convient dans le contexte où il apparaît.

Certains mots vont bien ensemble; il s'agit de collocations.

Certains mots sont fréquemment confondus, notamment par calque sur le français. Ainsi un texte « does not speak about » mais « deals with / focuses on / is about... »; une politique « does not arise » mais « is adopted / introduced... » alors que « problems, controversies arise from... »; les prix ne sont pas « cheap » mais « low », pas « expensive » mais « high » alors qu'un objet peut l'être...

Voici une liste non exhaustive de **mots souvent confondus**:

- critique: critic, criticism, critical
- économique: economic, economical
- bien, bon: right, good, well
- politique: politics, policy, political, politician
- laisser: let, leave
- attendre: wait for, expect sb to
- rester: remain, be left, stay
- toujours, encore, déjà: already, still, (not) yet, again, always
- arriver: arrive, happen, occur, take place
- apprendre: learn, teach
- comme: like, as, how
- devant: in front of, before, ahead, opposite, facing, (go) past
- il y a: ago, there + « be »
- jusqu'à: so far as, up to, until
- manquer: lack, miss, run short of
- mort: dead, death, die
- auteur: author, writer, journalist
- faire: make, do
- gagner: earn, win, gain
- scientifique: scientist, scientific

Parfois on a **le choix entre plusieurs mots**. Le plus précis est souvent le bon.

Au lieu de :	**On peut penser à :**
people	citizens, inhabitants, taxpayers, the man-in-the-street…
say	argue, state, imply, point out…
talk	mention, discuss, deal with…
think	suppose, assume, consider, hold, feel, reckon…
lead	rule (a country), implement (a policy), wage (a war), run (a company)…
provoke	bring about (a catastrophe), give rise to (a controversy), entail or be responsible for (a problem), trigger off (a conflict)…
give	provide (someone with information), grant (someone permission), bring (benefits), supply…

Les **adjectifs « good », « bad », « big », « little », « strong » et « important »** sont souvent utilisés de manière erronée ou fade. Voici des mots plus précis ou valides en leur lieu et place :

- **good** : positive (consequence), beneficial (effect), tasty or fresh (food), right (amount, price), valid (excuse, reason), sensible (advice), well thought-out (solution), grand (house, idea, scheme, style, scale), great (effort, friend, surprise, voice, holidays, news), marvellous (idea), nice (idea, person, home, weather, day, food), becoming (clothes, style)…
- **bad** : negative (consequence), detrimental (effect), disgusting or repelling (food, smell, behaviour), atrocious (crime), awful (weather, headache), appalling (conditions), disgraceful (behaviour, reaction), wrong (figure), harmful (influence), poor (results, quantity, taste, weather, performance), dreadful (crime), frightful (wound, time), degrading (treatment), rude (language, behaviour, remarks), sloppy or slipshod (style, piece of work), trite (idea)…
- **big** : large (amount, number), substantial (rise, increase), high (level, price, ratio), sweeping (change, reform), leading (company)…
- **little** : small (town), young (brother), tiny (flat), short (trip), minor (consequence)…
- **strong** : fierce (controversy), drastic (measure), proficient at (a subject), sharp (voice), compelling (desire, argument, book, film), graphic (details), heavy-handed (person, treatment, compliment), flashy (clothes, car)…
- **important** : large (number, proportion, amount), sharp / significant (rise, fall), serious/major (problem, issue, crisis), fast (growth), radical

(change), critical (stage / situation / condition), historic (event), vital (role), crucial (point), fierce (controversy), leading (firms, businessman, politician), influential (person),

Enfin, bien entendu, il faut prendre garde aux **faux-amis**. Des exemples de fautes fréquentes :

- actually / eventually / currently / nowadays,
- affirm / assert / claim / maintain,
- aid / help,
- apparition / appearance / emergence,
- apply / implement / enforce,
- assist / attend,
- ensure / assure / insure / check,
- advantage / benefit,
- advocate / lawyer,
- benefit / profit,
- country / campaign,
- chance / luck / likelihood,
- cite / quote / mention,
- condemn / sentence,
- know / have / be faced with / go through / experience,
- side / hand,
- believe / think,
- demand / ask / question,
- in effect / in fact / actually,
- enterprise / company / firm / business,
- eventual / potential / possible,
- service / favour,
- ignore / not to know / be unaware of,
- issue / outcome,
- measure / extent,
- middle / environment / world / background / medium,
- occasion / opportunity / second-hand,
- remark / note / notice,
- part / party / number / extent,

- pass / take,
- precise / specify,
- pretend / claim,
- profit / take advantage of,
- publicity / advertising / advertisement,
- photography / photograph / photographer,
- realise / carry out / make / direct,
- research / search,
- rentable / profitable,
- represent / be / account for,
- society / company,
- support / bear / stand,
- term / word / end,
- touch / affect / hit / receive,
- common / widespread…

3. Restitution des informations nécessaires

Attention !!! Aucune digression, aucune opinion, aucun commentaire, aucune information ajoutée au dossier proposé ne sont tolérés.

La première exigence est que les informations principales soient clairement exposées, les grandes lignes données. Est bonifié un ensemble précis et complet, perspicace, hiérarchisé et fiable. Le lecteur peut alors se forger une bonne idée sans avoir à lire le dossier d'origine.

4. Structuration, confrontation des documents et enchaînement ordonné

Se contenter d'écrire des résumés successifs est à proscrire.

Il faut éviter de présenter une synthèse mal organisée, articulée de façon sommaire et de se répéter.

La confrontation des documents doit être claire et faire apparaître les points de convergence et/ou de divergence. Si des opinions sont exprimées, il faut faire apparaître qui en est l'auteur. Les idées doivent être développées de manière égale mais en fonction de leur importance dans le dossier. La structure et l'enchaînement logique des idées doit permettre d'apporter une réponse claire à la problématique posée.

Sont bonifiées la clarté, des transitions solides et cohérentes, une structure logique, une bonne argumentation des idées.

a. Quelques mots de liaison

➡ Cause et conséquence

as, since = comme, parce que, puisque, étant donné que, vu que
because = car, parce que
on account of, because of = à cause de
owing to = en raison de
consequently = par conséquent
that's why = c'est pourquoi
therefore, as a result, hence = en conséquence

➡ But

for + nom
in order to, so as to, (not) to + proposition infinitive
so that + proposition

➡ Condition et hypothèse

nevertheless = néanmoins
even if = même si
even though = bien que
if = si
in case + should = au cas où
so long as = tant que
provided = pourvu que, à condition que
unless = à moins que
whether = si oui ou non

➡ Crainte

for fear that, lest = de peur que

➡ Concession, opposition, contraste

all the same = malgré tout
though = pourtant
despite, in spite of + groupe nominal = en dépit de
however, yet = cependant, pourtant
no matter how + adjectif ou adverbe = avoir beau
unlike, contrary to = contrairement à, à la différence de
but = mais
instead of + verbe en -ing = au lieu de
although = bien que
whereas = tandis que

➡ Temps

after = après que
as = comme, tandis que
as long as = tant que
as soon as = aussitôt que
before = avant que
by the time = d'ici à ce que
now that = maintenant que
once = une fois que
since = depuis que
till, until = jusqu'à ce que
when = quand
whenever = à chaque fois que
while = pendant que

b. Concision

Une synthèse, par définition, se doit de dénoter un esprit de concision. La langue anglaise s'y prête tout particulièrement puisqu'elle est plus concise que le français. Par exemple, les compléments circonstanciels de manière du français correspondent souvent à de simples adverbes, les tournures impersonnelles de probabilité à des modaux. Ou encore, les mots composés sont un excellent moyen de donner des informations en peu de mots (« state-owned », « poverty-stricken », « thought-provoking », « culturally-dependent », « home-made », etc.) mais il ne faut pas en abuser.

Évitez les circonlocutions qui sont superfétatoires, du type « according to Mr So-and-So » (Mr So-and-So says…) de même que les éléments redondants, voire les pléonasmes (« something costs a lot of money », « of money » n'ajoute rien).

À titre d'exemple, « be able to » peut être avantageusement remplacé par « can », « be maybe » par « may be », « first and foremost » par « first », « little by little » par « gradually », « more and more » par « progressively », « in the end » par « eventually », « be due to the fact that » par « be the result of », « in this way » par « thus », « in the same way » par « likewise », « in fact » par « actually », « in theory » par « theoretically », etc.

NB : voir chapitre 3, 3.b. exercice I.

5. Titre, problématisation introductive et sources

Un titre clair, pertinent et informatif doit chapeauter le corps de la synthèse. Ce n'est pas un article de presse ; il faut donc s'abstenir d'un titre accrocheur qui serait elliptique et/ou sibyllin.

L'introduction doit comporter une problématique claire et pertinente et mentionner correctement les sources de manière adroite.

Sont bonifiés la pertinence, la richesse, la concision et la clarté.

Partie II

Entraînements et sujets d'annales

File 1

Plastics

I. Ready

Documents

1. "Handling plastics", adapted from *The Guardian*, 2008
2. "Plastic is a sea life menace", adapted from *The Independent*, 2008
3. "Defending the plastic bag", adapted from *The International Herald Tribune*, 2009
4. "A revival", adapted from *The Economist*, 2010
5. An excerpt from *The Terrible Privacy of Maxwell Sim*, Jonathan Coe, 2010

Rédiger en anglais et en 400 mots une synthèse des documents proposés. Vous indiquerez avec précision à la fin de votre synthèse le nombre de mots qu'elle comporte. Un écart de 10 % en plus ou en moins sera accepté. Votre synthèse comportera un titre comptabilisé dans le nombre de mots.

Document 1

Handling plastics

Adapted from *The Guardian,* February 2008

While China, a world emerging superpower, is facing more and more environmental hazards, the mere issue of plastic bags may seem irrelevant, but aesthetics is not the key point. When discarded plastic bags are a burden on waterways, sewers and soil.

So as one of its new year's resolutions China has pledged to put a stop to its 30bn-a-day habit, and to ban the use of free and flimsy plastic bags by introducing charges. As of June this year plastic bags must be paid for, and they will be banned from all public transport, airports and scenic places.

The thing is, plastic is terrific. Why? Its multiple possible uses, its durability, its being waterproof, practical and truly cheap are among its appealing advantages. But these benefits can turn out to be doubled-edged as with the case in point of the sheer persistence of plastic bags.

The thicker they are, the longer it takes plastic bags to break down – up to a millennium. Their burning leads to toxic gases being released while the stagnant pools they create are the ideal ground for malaria to thrive in mosquitoes; and should animals consume them, which they well might, that is a cause of suffocation or indigestion.

Better waste management in Europe than in the developing world makes the threat of plastic bags less material there. China's situation is perhaps better reflected by experiences in African places. [...]

The United Nations Environment Programme (UNEP) reckons the South African ban to be effective – South Africans used to consume some eight billion plastic bags on a yearly basis. Below-30-micron-thick bags have been totally banned as they can easily blow away and turn out to be hard to recycle. There is less littering consequently now. A charge is in place and if people do not comply with the ban, penalties are really tough: fines and even prison sentences.

Before regulation was introduced in South Africa, the cost of producing, delivering and distributing plastic bags was concealed in food prices, so even if customers did not want a bag, they would pay for it. Now they can choose to pay and have a bag or not to pay – and UNEP reports that consumers have therefore benefited from lower food prices.

Nonetheless, consumers are still more prone to choosing plastic bags than paper ones or boxes. It seems that we are addicted. What remains to be seen is whether China can get rid of the habit, or find a truly fantastic – and biodegradable – plastic bag.

➡ Document 2

Plastic is a sea life menace

Adapted from *The Independent*, February 2008

When an albatross died on a Pacific Island and its stomach was investigated, its contents were fairly astonishing: a cigarette lighter, a toothbrush, a toy robot and a tampon applicator. The poor chick had gulped a very fishy assortment of household objects instead of its usual healthy diet.

Unfortunately this is not an isolated case: thousands of seabirds have ingested plastic debris and died. This type of marine pollution is so widespread that even very remote places are affected. [...]

Birds are not the only ones to suffer. Turtles, whales, seals and sea lions have all eaten plastic. But the most obnoxious problem may be hidden at the end of the food chain.

Small sand-hoppers, barnacles and lugworms have also been found to have ingested tiny fragments of plastic, some of which are thinner than a human hair. [...]

The reason why plastic is so ubiquitous in our homes and offices, of course, explains why it builds up in the wider environment: it is resilient and takes years to break down into its constituent molecules.

This resilience is even truer in seas and oceans as the water generally protects plastic from the ultra-violet light which acts in the breaking-down process.

Experts actually reckon that all the plastic that was dumped into the sea – even decades ago – is still there now, either floating around or lying on the seabed where it is likely to be eaten up by passing sea-creatures, be they birds, fish or mammals.

And yet plastic consumption is set to continue its expansion – by as much as a third in the space of a single decade in the case of each north-American consumer – while the solution to the problem of wildlife-jeopardising plastic is to cut our consumption and to stop treating plastic as harmless. Indeed there is now a case for it to be treated as a potentially toxic waste product with the stiffest sanctions for its desultory disposal.

➡ Document 3

Defending the plastic bag

Adapted from *The International Herald Tribune*, February 2009

Plastic bags have become unfashionable in many cities which have prohibited, taxed or limited their use. Even developing countries, where more pressing needs, jobs for example, often outweigh nobler aims, are adopting similar measures. Just last June, New Delhi passed a preliminary ban imposing a five-year jail term or a fine of 100,000 rupees, or about $2,050, on anyone caught carrying or handing out plastic bags.

Yet, last week, the city hosted the meeting of 67,000 plastics executives from around the world. While looking at new products and attending seminars, they would complain about the unfair prejudice they say plastic is subject to. "Politicians have gone overboard," said Arvind Mehta, president of the trade group sponsoring the conference. "Our industry is facing a problem, and we have to fight." Using the same argument that the American firearms lobby claim, he said that it's not the plastic bag that causes the problems but rather the person who uses it.

Some 100 billion plastic bags are sold a year in the world. Most US cities, unlike San Francisco that has completely banned them, have abandoned such plans. Another example: Ireland. There is simply a tax on plastic bags there because industry groups have lobbied against an outright ban. However, the "no plastic bag" movement gathers momentum around the world as big retailers promise to cut back and consumers turn to paper and canvas bags.

With the threat of a prison sentence, in New Delhi, many consumers and shopkeepers have been very careful in recent weeks and used cardboard boxes and baskets instead of plastic bags. In some countries, including South Africa and China, the thinnest plastic bags have been banned in favor of thicker, reusable plastic bags, and recycling of old bags into new ones is being encouraged.

But the people who attend the New Delhi conference say the plastic bag proves hard to replace as there is not always a substitute; for instance when it rains, paper bags are disastrous. They argue governments should be encouraging recycling rather than banning bags. Of the 350 tons of plastic bags a manufacturer makes a year, 250 tons are made from recycled material. Another crucial point is that plastic manufacturing is a big employer – one million Indian people work in this sector. The country is a top manufacturer of plastic products, and Indian executives predict that it will grow to be the third-largest consumer of plastic goods by 2010, behind the United States and China.

But even industry executives acknowledge that plastic bags are not environmentally-friendly as they take hundreds of year to break down and that biodegradable bags are expensive. "Western countries should find a way to convert them back to oil," Mehta said.

➠ Document 4

There and back again
An old idea may help solve the problem of plastic waste

Adapted from *The Economist,* Oct 28th 2010

PLASTICS were once regarded as wonder-materials. They are still ubiquitous, but find less favour than they used to because of the very stability and persistence that won them applause in the first place. Many people now consider them as a nuisance and a threat.

That is why biodegradable plastics are being researched into. One possibility has recently been explored by David Schiraldi of Case Western Reserve University, in Ohio, and his colleagues. What they intend to do is to revive the use of milk in producing plastics as that was the case more than a century ago.

What they actually suggest is using casein, the principal protein found in milk, and more particularly in the curds. In 1889 a French chemist called Jean-Jacques Trillat discovered that if casein is treated with formaldehyde the result is a hard, shiny substance that does well as a substitute for materials like ivory and tortoiseshell. […] However, casein-based plastic of this sort is too brittle for it to be easily used. It was eventually superseded by the modern, petrochemical variety, and manufacture stopped altogether by the 1970s.

These days the thought of reviving it, though, is strengthening again because the fact that it could be chewed up by bacteria, since it is mostly made of proteins, is regarded as a virtue—if only the structural weakness could be overcome. Dr Schiraldi's approach does this by using a silicate clay called sodium montmorillonite as a skeleton that holds the plastic together.

[…]

The researchers report in *Biomacromolecules* that their new material matches the stiffness, strength and compressibility of expanded polystyrene […]. However, unlike polystyrene, it goes away once it has been dumped. An initial experiment suggested that 20% of it vanished within 18 days in a dump-like environment. […]

Document 5

The Terrible Privacy of Maxwell Sim

Jonathan Coe, 2010, ch9

[Trevor said,] "Alan saw what the majors were doing wrong. He saw where the future lies: green toothbrushes."

"Green?" I said, puzzled.

"I don't mean the colour, Max. We're talking about sustainable energy, renewable sources. Let me ask you – where do you think most toothbrushes are made?"

"China?"

"Correct. And what are they made of?"

"Plastic?"

"Right again. And what are the bristles made of?"

I could never answer questions like this. "I don't know… Something synthetic?"

"Exactly. Nylon, to be precise. Now what does that sound like to you? To me, it sounds like a recipe for environmental disaster. Dentists recommend that we change toothbrushes every three months. Four times a year. That means you're going to get through about three hundred toothbrushes in your lifetime. Worse than that, it means that in the UK alone, we probably throw away about two hundred million toothbrushes every year. Good for the big corporations, of course – it means people have to keep buying new ones. But that's old-style thinking, Max. You can't put sales ahead of the environment any more. For the sake of humanity, we're all got to change our tune. The profit motive has to play second fiddle. [...] Now – Alan knew the solutions weren't difficult to find. [...] Option number one [...] a wooden toothbrush. [...] Made from sustainable wood, of course – one hundred percent European pine. No damage to the rainforests here. And when you've finished with it, you can throw it on the fire, or shred it and put it in the compost."

[...] "What are the bristles made of?" I asked.

"Boar-hair," said Trevor.

2. Steady

a. Tableau de synthèse

Cf. page suivante.

b. Theme: plastic

- **Question:** What can be done to stop the plastic threat?
- **Outline:** From different points of view:
  - Manufacturers
  - Consumers
  - Governments and organizations
  - The environment

Handling plastic ***The Guardian*, 2008**	**Plastic is a sea life menace** ***The Independent*, 2008**	**Defending the plastic bag** ***The IHT*, 2009**	**A revival** ***The Economist*, 2010**	***The Terrible Privacy…*** **J. Coe, 2010**
China and South Africa Advantages of plastics: cheap, versatile, durable, waterproof, convenient Downsides of plastics: persistent, toxic-gas releasing, disrupt waterways, clog sewers, choke soil, create malaria-inducing stagnant pools, life-threatening for animals Solutions: a) alternatives: creating biodegradable plastic bags; b) charges and bans: Chinese ban on flimsy bags and charges, South African ban of under-30-micron-thick bags + charges, fines and imprisonment for non-compliance → lower food prices as plastic used to be included in prices	Seas Advantages of plastics: resilient, persistent, at least 50-year-old → ubiquitous in homes and offices Downsides of plastics: the scourge of sea life as birds, fish, mammals and crustaceans ingest plastic bits and die from it. Stomachs of dead birds bear witness to that → the whole sea food chain is contaminated and jeopardised. Cause: UV don't operate deep sea; we consume more and more plastics Solutions: decrease consumption, beware of plastic; sanctions for getting rid of it thoughtlessly	Plastics executives' meeting in New Delhi Laws in New Delhi, the US, South Africa, Ireland, China 100 bn plastic bags a year worldwide Advantages of plastics: waterproof, persistent, source of jobs Downsides of plastics: longevity → bad for the environment Solutions: a) alternatives: paper and canvas bags, expensive biodegradable plastics; b) charges and bans: Indian bans and fines, former bans in the US esp. San Francisco, Irish tax, Indian jail time; c) means: recycling, using only thick bags and reusable bags People involved: manufacturers, consumers, governments and local authorities (should encourage recycling according to makers) Top ranking consumers: the US, China, India Argument: consumers are to blame not plastic itself	Advantages of plastics: persistent, strong → ubiquitous Downsides of plastics: threat to the environment Solutions: alternatives: biodegradable alternative, made from milk casein + a silicate clay – a 19th century invention revived	Example of plastic toothbrushes; very environmentally unfriendly but much used → waste; profit-making firms Solution: wooden toothbrushes

3. Go

Tackling the plastic issue

Plastics are both praised and decried but undeniably non-environmentally-friendly. What can be realistically and wisely done to stop the threat they pose to the environment? This question is answered by a 2008 *Guardian* article dealing with the Chinese and South African situations, a 2008 *Independent* paper focusing on plastic-polluted seas, a 2009 *International Herald Tribune* column highlighting manufacturers' views, a 2010 *Economist* article pointing at a new type of plastic and an excerpt from one of Jonathan Coe's novels condemning plastic. Different points of views and stances are thus expressed.

The environment must complain about plastics as they threaten it. Indeed not only do they take a long time to break down as they are persistent – with a minimum 50-year lifespan – but meanwhile they release noxious gases and entail the creation of malaria-provoking stagnant pools, stifle soils, block sewers, and disrupt waterways and UV-free deep-sea and shallower-sea life, whereby the whole sea food chain gets contaminated and jeopardised as bird innards bear witness to. Animal lives are thus endangered.

Nonetheless, plastic manufacturers – as those who gathered and met in New Delhi in 2009 – argue that plastic is blame-free but consumers are not, so recycling should be encouraged. They also remind opponents that the plastic industry does create jobs as it is profitable with 100bn plastic bags used a year worldwide. Indeed consumers are also ubiquitous – the Americans, Chinese and Indians rank first – and consumption has been increasing. Toothbrushes are a case in point for J. Coe. Indeed generally speaking plastic has many possible uses, is very convenient, waterproof and cheap.

Governments, local authorities and organisations do not seem to be convinced by such arguments as more and more of them are introducing measures to eradicate plastic bags. There are or were outright bans on the thinnest ones in China, South Africa, India and San Francisco, USA, for instance. India has also introduced fines and jail sentences for non-compliance. Ireland put taxes on such bags. These measures may even make food prices lower as plastic used to be factored in. Alternatives are also being considered as biodegradable plastic bags – though expensive but with one model reviving a 19th century milk-casein-based invention – and paper and canvas bags or thick reusable bags. *The Independent* adds that people should be more aware of plastic and there should be sanctions for getting rid of it thoughtlessly. The case of toothbrushes could be solved by using wood instead of plastic for handles, writes J. Coe humourously.

There is obviously no shortage of ideas in the plastic war.

426 words

File 2

The special relationship

I. Ready

➡ Documents

1. Beginning of Obama's speech to UK Parliament on 25 May 2011
2. What I call special, adapted from *The Independent*, 25 May 2011
3. Article in *The Times*, written by B. Obama & D. Cameron
4. Cartoon from *The Guardian*, 26 May 2011

Rédiger en anglais et en 500 mots environ une synthèse des documents proposés. Vous indiquerez avec précision à la fin de votre synthèse le nombre de mots qu'elle comporte. Un écart de 10 % en plus ou en moins sera accepté. Votre synthèse comportera un titre comptabilisé dans le nombre de mots.

➡ Document 1

Beginning of Obama's speech to UK Parliament on 25 May 2011

As part of a state visit, US President Barack Obama gave a keynote address to both houses of the British Parliament, gathered at London's Westminster Hall on 25 May 2011.

"My Lord Chancellor, Mr Speaker, Mr Prime Minister, my Lords, and Members of the House of Commons:

"[...] I've come here today to reaffirm one of the oldest, one of the strongest alliances the world has ever known. It has long been said that the United States and the United Kingdom share a special relationship.

"And since we also share an especially active press corps, that relationship is often analysed and over-analysed for the slightest hint of stress or strain.

"Of course, all relationships have their ups and downs. Admittedly, ours got off on the wrong foot with a small scrape about tea and taxes.

"There may have also been some hurt feelings when the White House was set on fire during the War of 1812. But fortunately, it's been smooth sailing ever since!

"The reason for this close friendship doesn't just have to do with our shared history, our shared heritage; our ties of language and culture; or even the strong partnership between our governments. Our relationship is special because of the values and beliefs that have united our people through the ages.

"Centuries ago, when kings, emperors, and warlords reigned over much of the world, it was the English who first spelled out the rights and liberties of man in the Magna Carta.

"It was here, in this very hall, where the rule of law first developed, courts were established, disputes were settled, and citizens came to petition their leaders.

"Over time, the people of this nation waged a long and sometimes bloody struggle to expand and secure their freedom from the crown. Propelled by the ideals of the Enlightenment, they would ultimately forge an English Bill of Rights, and invest the power to govern in an elected parliament that's gathered here today.

"What began on this island would inspire millions throughout the continent of Europe and across the world.

"But perhaps no-one drew greater inspiration from these notions of freedom than your rabble-rousing colonists on the other side of the Atlantic. As Winston Churchill said, the '... Magna Carta, the Bill of Rights, the Habeas Corpus, trial by jury, and English common law find their most famous expression in the American Declaration of Independence'.

"For both of our nations, living up to the ideals enshrined in these founding documents has sometimes been difficult, has always been a work in progress.

"The path has never been perfect. But through the struggles of slaves and immigrants; women and ethnic minorities; former colonies and persecuted religions, we have learned better than most that the longing for freedom and human dignity is not English or American or Western – it is universal, and it beats in every heart.

"Perhaps that's why there are few nations that stand firmer, speak louder, and fight harder to defend democratic values around the world than the United States and the United Kingdom.

"We are the allies who landed at Omaha and Gold; who sacrificed side by side to free a continent from the march of tyranny, and help prosperity flourish from the ruins of war. And with the founding of Nato – a British idea – we joined a transatlantic alliance that has ensured our security for over half a century.

"Together with our allies, we forged a lasting peace from a Cold War. When the Iron Curtain lifted, we expanded our alliance to include the nations of Central and Eastern Europe, and built new bridges to Russia and the former states of the Soviet Union. And when there was strife in the Balkans, we worked together to keep the peace.

"Today, after a difficult decade that began with war and ended in recession, our nations have arrived at a pivotal moment once more. A global economy that once stood on the brink of depression is now stable and recovering.

"After years of conflict, the United States has removed 100,000 troops from Iraq, the United Kingdom has removed its forces, and our combat mission there has ended. In Afghanistan, we have broken the Taliban's momentum, and will soon begin a transition to Afghan lead.

"And nearly 10 years after 9/11, we have disrupted terrorist networks and dealt al-Qaeda a huge blow by killing its leader – Osama bin Laden.

"Together, we have met great challenges. But as we enter this new chapter in our shared history, profound challenges stretch before us.

"In a world where the prosperity of all nations is now inextricably linked, a new era of co-operation is required to ensure the growth and stability of the global economy.

"As new threats spread across borders and oceans, we must dismantle terrorist networks and stop the spread of nuclear weapons; confront climate change and combat famine and disease. And as a revolution races through the streets of the Middle East and North Africa, the entire world has a stake in the aspirations of a generation that longs to determine its own destiny.

"These challenges come at a time when the international order has already been reshaped for a new century. Countries like China, India, and Brazil are growing by leaps and bounds. We should welcome this development, for it has lifted hundreds of millions from poverty around the globe, and created new markets and opportunities for our own nations.

"And yet, as this rapid change has taken place, it has become fashionable in some quarters to question whether the rise of these nations will accompany the decline of American and European influence around the world. Perhaps, the argument goes, these nations represent the future, and the time for our leadership has passed.

"That argument is wrong. The time for our leadership is now. It was the United States and the United Kingdom, and our democratic allies, that shaped a world in which new nations could emerge and individuals could thrive. And even as more nations take on the responsibilities of global leadership, our alliance will remain indispensable to the goal of a century that is more peaceful, more prosperous and more just."

➡ Document 2

What I call special

Wednesday 25 May 2011 – adapted from *The Independent*

Yesterday, two middle-aged men declared that they have a relationship that is not only special but essential. Honestly, I'm not sure that anyone cares about it or that the choice of adjectives and adverbs matters.

Whoever ghost-wrote the piece by Barack Obama and David Cameron in yesterday's Times was keen to point out that the President of the world's only superpower and the Prime Minister of a medium-sized country in Europe had an awful lot in common. They both "came of age during the 1980s". They both "look at the world in a similar way". They both (he or she didn't quite say, but might have) wear nice suits and ties. One, the author of the piece didn't say, believes in fiscal stimulus, and the other believes in austerity. One believes in expanding the state. The other believes in cutting it. But it was neither the time nor the place to play differences up, on the contrary.

There is a special relationship, though. Not between Barack Obama and David Cameron, nor between their countries. There is a special relationship between Barack Obama and the Queen, or as it was phrased in an interview of the US President on Sunday as Obama's "chemistry" with the Queen. [...]

What a week both have had. The Queen braved some of the tightest security the country has ever seen to visit, for the first time, Ireland. Obama braved some of the tightest security the country has ever seen to visit, for the first time, Ireland. The Queen went down a treat. Obama went down a treat. The Queen talked about history. Obama talked about history. [...]

The Queen won over 95 per cent of the population of [the] country [...] because they could see who she was. They could see that she was a dutiful, hard-working, intelligent woman who doesn't suffer fools gladly, and who smiles when she wants to, and doesn't when she doesn't. They could see, in other words, that she was the real McCoy.

Obama is, if not Obama, also the real McCoy. He doesn't smile when he doesn't want to. He doesn't, or at least he doesn't seem to, say things he doesn't mean. He doesn't go for big displays of emotion. [...] Like the Queen, he is careful and steady. Like the Queen, too, he's magnetic. [...] He's the most powerful man in the world. But he has the quality that she has, too. It has something to do with knowing who you are, and something to do with calm. [...]

Over almost six decades now, the Queen has met plenty of heads of state and visited plenty of countries as she has been to all the member countries of the Commonwealth which used to be the British Empire. During her reign, she has watched 82 colonies turn themselves into independent states (through joy, hardships or bloody battles). This is a woman who knows about history. This is a woman who knows that change takes time.

Barack Obama also knows that change takes time. [...] You can't make a collapsing economy suddenly bloom and flourish with jobs for everyone and revive extinct industries. You can't wean your car-loving voters off oil in the twinkle of an eye. You can't suddenly rewrite the politics of the Middle East.

But you can [...] pass a stunning healthcare bill to provide access for 32 million Americans. You can stimulate the economy. You can create jobs. You can reform Wall Street. [...]. And you can track down, and kill, a mass murderer. [...]

"Most politicians," said Obama in the interview, "spend their time talking, rather than listening. That," he said, "is a habit that I try to break." I'm sure the Queen would agree. I'm sure she's also proud of him.

➡ Document 3

Barack Obama and David Cameron

"Both of us came of age during the 1980s.

Like so many others, we recall a turbulent decade that began with armies confronting each other across a divided Europe and ended with the Berlin Wall coming down, millions freed from the shackles of communism and human dignity extended across the continent.

The Cold War reached this conclusion because of the actions of many brave individuals and many strong nations, but we saw how the bond between our two countries – and our two leaders at the time – proved such a vital catalyst for change. It reminded us that when the United States and Britain stand together, our people and people around the world can become more secure and more prosperous.

And that is the key to our relationship. Yes, it is founded on a deep emotional connection, by sentiment and ties of people and culture. But the reason it thrives, the reason why this is such a natural partnership, is because it advances our common interests and shared values. It is a perfect alignment of what we both need and what we both believe. And the reason it remains strong is because it delivers time and again. Ours is not just a special relationship, it is an essential relationship – for us and for the world.

So as we meet today, facing immense economic, social and strategic challenges, it is natural that once again our two nations join together in common cause. Today the foundations of our partnership are rock solid. Our servicemen and women serve alongside one another [...].

And we can honestly say that despite being two leaders from two different political traditions, we see eye to eye. We look at the world in a similar way, share the same concerns and see the same strategic possibilities. So we will build on the relationship between the UK and US, working closely together on areas of common interest to make it stronger still. [...]"

➡ Document 4

Cartoon – Gary Barker

guardian.co.uk, Thursday 26 May 2011

2. Steady

a. Tableau de synthèse

Cf. page suivante.

b. Theme: the relationship between the USA and the UK

- **Question:** What can be said to be special about the relationship between the US & the UK?
- **Outline:**
  - I. The two countries
    - a. History
    - b. Values, beliefs, interests
    - c. Militarily
    - d. World leadership
  - II. Their leaders
    - a. Obama and Elizabeth II
    - b. Obama and Cameron

Obama's speech in Parliament, London, 25 May 2011	What I call special, 25 May 2011, *The Independent*	B. Obama & D. Cameron's joint paper, 24 May 2011, *The Times*	Cartoon, Gary Barker, *The Guardian*, 26 May 2011
Though too much hype there is a special relationship between US & UK, yes	Criticism of joint paper & stress on special relationship & because more differences than similarities between the 2 Special relationship between Obama & the Queen	A special relationship between the 2 men & their countries because of similarities	Cameron & the Obamas in front of 10 Downing Street Pun on the **special** relationship
Historically: ups & downs but shared heritage, culture, language & governmental partnership	Obama & Elizabeth II: long reign & aware any kind of change takes time		Cameron-UK a mere lackey to the Obamas-US, carrying (out) US/common foreign policies
Values & beliefs in common: established first by the Brits & best implemented by the US (Magna Carta, Parliament, freedom…) struggling to live up to those ideals	Political & political differences → Obama & Cameron	US/UK: common interests & values despite political differences US/UK & Obama/Cameron: special relationship based on emotions, cultural & personal individual ties	
Military & diplomatic collaboration since WWII → peace & prosperity		Common stand has proved great for the world & their peoples – security & prosperity Military collaboration, same foreign policy	An unbalanced relationship
Further global challenges ahead must be faced with allies but still world leaders despite other nations' rise		An effective strong special relationship New challenges so natural to act together	
	Obama & Elizabeth II: successful though tough visit to Ireland; talk about history; "the real McCoy" i.e. authentic & honest; careful, steady, charismatic; great achievers; good listeners	Obama & Cameron: same generation, same reminiscences (Cold War & its end)	

3. Go

Friends or master and servant?

Barack Obama's May 2011 visit to the United Kingdom once more led to endless talk and writing about the UK/US special relationship. But how special is it? What can define it? Is it balanced? What did and will it achieve? That is what is at stake in Obama's speech to the British Parliament, his *Times* column, co-authored with David Cameron, an article from *The Independent* and a British press cartoon, all published during that visit, focusing broadly on the too much hyped relationship between the two countries and more narrowly on the one between their heads of state.

Obama's speech insists first on the two countries' shared history which led to common heritage, language and culture despite some fighting too. Both statesmen also underline, not only the emotional and individual ties, but the great achievements their governmental partnership made for their own peoples and the world, which they believe entitles them to still be world leaders despite the rise of new nations facing new global challenges with their allies. Indeed their past military and diplomatic collaboration since WWII had ensured world peace and economic prosperity. So the US/UK relationship is strong because fruitful. The President, however, also emphasises the common values, beliefs and needs of the two countries as the strong basis of their relationship together with the Prime Minister. These universal ideals, he says, were invented by the Brits (Magna Carta, power of the people, freedom) and best implemented by the US, though having struggled to live up to them.

Yet the historical connection is one which Obama and Cameron are personally aware of too as they belong to the same generation and therefore both have the Cold War in mind as a reminder of a close relationship between their nations, according to *The Independent* article. It nevertheless, also criticises *The Times* paper for over-emphasising the similarities between the two statesmen, downplaying their political differences and their diverging economic ideas. Likewise the cartoon denounces their relationship as superficial, hypocritical and unbalanced. *The Guardian* cartoonist portrays David Cameron as the presidential couple's lackey, merely useful to help carry out the American military foreign policy instead of a joint action on an equal footing. It would not be those two men who would have a special relationship, that is, those who could be put in an equation, but rather Obama and the Queen. *The Independent* columnist relates how both have successfully recently visited Ireland-despite security issues-where both talked about history, how both are genuine, honest people, careful, steady and charismatic statespeople. Both are aware of the time requirement for changing things as **she** has had an eventful reign and **he** has faced, and is facing, economic, environmental, diplomatic and domestic challenges. But both have achieved great things during their term of office as they must be good listeners.

The special relationship between the US and Britain consequently would be mostly a question of individuals to reach equilibrium as today, in spite of a shared past and common values and publicly-voiced interests, their joint foreign policy might not reflect such a balance.

515 words

File 3

Space debris

I. Ready

Documents

- Orbiting junk – *The NYTimes* – Feb 2007
- Inevitable space collisions – *The Washington Post* – Feb 2009
- More space junk... – *The Washington Post* – 13 Jan 2012
- A vacuum cleaner – *www.globalpost.com* – 15 Feb 2012
- Low earth orbit image, NASA

Rédiger en anglais et en 500 mots une synthèse des documents proposés. Vous indiquerez avec précision à la fin de votre synthèse le nombre de mots qu'elle comporte. Un écart de 10 % en plus ou en moins sera accepté. Votre synthèse comportera un titre comptabilisé dans le nombre de mots.

Document 1

Orbiting Junk, from nuisance to threat

Adapted from *The New York Times,* February 2007

The concern is not new but the likelihood is getting closer and the urgency more acute. Indeed as early this year the federal list of detectable objects in space (10 centimeters wide or large) reached 10,000 while over the last few years scientists anxiously agreed to say that the number of objects in orbit had exceeded a critical mass so that one day a speeding piece of debris might well crash into a big spacecraft into hundreds of pieces, starting a chain reaction.

And that is likely to start sooner than forecast earlier because of China's test on January 11 of an anti-satellite rocket that shattered an old satellite into hundreds of large pieces. If experts' predictions materialize, very expensive advanced satellites could be at risk and mankind may no longer have the opportunity to reach for the stars.

[...]

An MIT expert working on the issue said China might have failed to realize the huge extent of the indirect hazards entailed by the test or its engineers might have failed to communicate those risks.

China, experts note, has 39 satellites of its own – many of them now facing a heightened risk of destruction.

Politically, China is in a delicate situation as it has been playing a growing role on the international stage to prevent space junk from proliferating. [...] In April, Beijing is to play host to the annual meeting of the advocacy group, known as the Inter-Agency Space Debris Coordination Committee. Donald J. Kessler, a former head of the orbital debris program at NASA and a pioneer analyst of the space threat, said Chinese officials at the forum would probably be somewhat embarrassed.

[...]

Cascade warnings began as early as 1978 when Mr Kessler and a NASA colleague wrote in the Journal of Geophysical Research that speeding junk would produce "an exponential increase in the number of objects with time, creating a belt of debris around the Earth."

[...]

If nothing is done, a kind of orbital crisis might happen. It is known as the Kessler Syndrome, after Mr. Kessler. It holds that the space around the Earth becomes so full of junk that launchings are almost impossible. Vehicles that have entered space would quickly be destroyed.

Mr Kessler said that to prevent that spacecraft will have to be more and more shielded, which will be more and more expensive. "Sooner or later it gets too expensive to do business in space," he declared.

Document 2

Inevitable space collisions

Adapted from *The Washington Post*, February 2009

Satellite 33442 – actually a tool bag, let slip by an astronaut by mistake last year – orbits the earth every 91 minutes, circling at an inclination of 56.1 degrees to the equator and gradually slowing down. It is supposed to fall into the atmosphere in late spring or summer and burn up.

Satellite 33442 is just one bit among the 18,000 pieces of orbital debris tracked by the US military. Yet last week the census of orbiting junk suddenly soared with another 600 bits, the initial estimate of the number of fragments from a stunning collision of two satellites high above Siberia.

Space is now similar to a dumping site of a civilization that heavily depends on satellites. That space garbage is becoming ever more threatening as it has put everything from the Hubble space telescope to communications satellites at risk of being struck by an object moving at hypervelocity.

The military's radar can spot objects as small as a baseball. This collision, however, may have produced many thousands of small, undetectable pieces of debris that would still carry enough kinetic punch at orbital velocities to damage or destroy a spacecraft. "We expect there will be tens or hundreds of thousands of pieces," said Nicholas Johnson, NASA's chief scientist for orbital debris.

All that is to be added to what has been accumulating in space for decades. For instance, in 2007, China's destroying one of its old satellites to show a new missile's capability meant another 2,500 detectable fragments up there.

[…]

According to some experts, some regions in space are now as polluted as Lake Erie used to be in the 1960s. Yet there is one major difference in that, at higher orbits (800 km and above), space cannot evacuate its contaminants very quickly as there is slight atmospheric drag. At lower orbits (about 322 km), atmospheric drag with the friction of air molecules slows down objects until they fall to Earth to burn up when they re-enter the atmosphere.

Space pollution can get worse over time, because objects strike one another and spew out smaller fragments, said David Wright, a physicist with the Union of Concerned Scientists. He warned of the danger of a runaway chain reaction, with junk smashing into junk and creating a fog of speeding detritus all around the planet. […]

In low earth orbit, satellites have been whizzing past one another without a glitch for years. But they don't do so as trucks on a road since they operate in three dimensions. Space is big, as the experts say. Thus the odds of any particular satellite hitting another are remote. But over time, with enough spacecraft, and enough pieces of spacecraft, the chances of a collision increase as it happened in 2007.

➠ Document 3

More space junk forecast with the crash of a Russian Mars probe

Adapted from *The Washington Post*, January 13, 2012

What went up is going to come down – and soon.

A failed Russian Mars probe stranded above Earth since November will plunge to its doom this weekend, likely on Sunday. […]

But predicting when and where space objects will fall is tricky. […] As a result the spacecraft, called Phobos-Grunt, could plummet back to Earth over North America, South America, Europe, Asia or even Australia.

"It's not possible to say where the thing is going to fall down," Heiner Klinkrad, head of the orbital debris office at the European Space Agency in Darmstadt, Germany, said in an interview on Friday.

Roscosmos, the Russian space agency, expects 500 pounds of the nearly 15-ton craft to survive reentry, with the rest burning up. According to its latest forecast, it should crash into the Atlantic Ocean but there is no certainty. As the craft drops lower and lower, its path will become more accurately predicted. […]

A joint statement issued on Friday by NASA and the Federal Emergency Management Agency said the agencies are "closely monitoring the situation and are taking all necessary precautions and preparations to be ready to support our federal, state and local partners in the unlikely event that there are impacts to the United States." […]

"In 50 years of modern spaceflight, we have not had one serious injury due to reentering space objects," Klinkrad said. […]

The problem of space junk has drawn increasing international attention. In 2007, the United Nations Committee on the Peaceful Uses of Outer Space adopted new guidelines for space-faring countries to minimize the dangers of space junk.

NASA now designs its satellites with thrusters so that they either fall into the ocean or are sent into higher orbits where they will remain.

The $163 million Mars probe in question was supposed to be a technological triumph for Russia as it was designed to go to one of the moons of Mars to collect a soil sample to be sent to Earth for investigation, something never attempted so far.

Instead, Phobos-Grunt has become a searing embarrassment. The high-profile blunder has enticed Russian space officials to offer weirder and weirder theories to account for the problem. […]

➡ Document 4

A vacuum cleaner for space junk?

Space debris is a huge, and costly, problem.
But don't worry: the Swiss are on it.

February 15, 2012 – adapted from http: //www.globalpost.com/dispatches/globalpost-blogs/macro/vacuum-cleaner-space-junk

Thousands of pieces of space junk are today orbiting our blue planet, at dizzying and dangerous speeds.

NASA alone tracks 16,000 pieces of this stuff every day.

So what happens when this debris collides with one of the 700 satellites that are up there tracking our weather, as well as powering our phones, televisions, GPS devices, and other things?

More space junk is created, increasing the likelihood of further collisions, which, in turn, creates even more space junk.

The cycle goes on and on, hurtling toward a chaotic and dystopian future of surging costs and deadly peril for astronauts.

There have been no reports of space junk ever hitting anyone on Earth, though.

Anyway don't worry. Scientists at the Swiss Space Center at EPFL today announced the launch of CleanSpace One, what they call a "project to develop and build the first installment of a family of satellites specially designed to clean up space debris."

In other words, they're planning to launch giant vacuum cleaners into space to suck up debris, and then safely send it back down to earth.

➡ Document 5

Clutter in the Heavens

http: //www.orbitaldebris.jsc.nasa.gov/photogallery/beehives.html#geo

LEO images: LEO stands for low Earth orbit and is the region of space within 2,000 km of the Earth's surface. It is the most concentrated area for orbital debris.

2. Steady

a. Tableau de synthèse

Cf. page suivante.

b. Theme: space pollution

- **Question:** Which steps should be taken to make space exploration sustainable given the increase in space debris and incidents?
- **Outline:**
  1. Facts: the evolution of space debris and the possible Kessler Syndrome albeit qualifications
  2. Specific incidents
  3. Solutions

Orbiting junk ***The NYTimes*, Feb. 2007**	**Inevitable space collisions** ***The Washington Post*, Feb. 2009**	**More space junk** ***The Washington Post*, Jan. 2012**	**A vacuum cleaner** **www.globalpost.com, Feb. 2012**	**Clutter in the heavens** **NASA, low earth orbit image**
Issue: 10,000 pieces of debris (2007) Specific case: Chinese satellite destruction, January 2007 → chain reaction expected sooner Reactions: a) Chinese mishandling, lack of forethought and communications although high stakes for themselves too; likely embarrassment at April 2007 Beijing Space debris meeting b) experts: worry. Warnings as early as 1978. Mr Kessler, a pioneer analyst → the Kessler Syndrome = runaway chain reaction Possible consequences: launchings impossible; increasingly expensive necessary spacecraft shielding → end of space exploration	Issue/explanations: 18,000 pieces of debris from tool-bags to telescopes to disused communications satellites (2009) Moving at huge speed High drag in low Earth orbit → reduced speed → falling to Earth &/or danger of a runaway chain reaction Low drag in high Earth orbit → ok Qualifications: space is big; small odds of satellite collisions Specific increases: 2009 two-satellite collision + 600; 2007 Chinese purposefully destroying a satellite of its own + 2,500	Issue: predicting whereabout on Earth Russian Mars probe Phobos-Grunt is to go down; embarrassment and weird Russian explanations Qualification: close monitoring and so far no Earth casualty Wider issue: space debris Solutions: 2007 guidelines; special designs to prevent reentry or to direct at oceans	Issue: space debris reported by NASA – expanding Consequences: communication jeoprdised, costs increased, astronauts in danger, vicious expansion Qualification: no Earth casualty Solution: Swiss CleanSpaceOne satellite to hoover space	LEO image – a very cluttered area

Tackling space pollution

The human new environment that space has become may also mean a new pollution field. Indeed that raises more specifically the question of which steps should be taken to make space exploration sustainable given the increase in debris – as can be observed on a NASA picture – and incidents. The latter include a Chinese one as reported by a 2007 *New York Times* article and a *Washington Post* paper that deals with a 2009 satellite-collision too but also the 2012 unknown trajectory of a Russian probe focused on by a January 2012 *Washington Post* article. Still a February 2012 globalpost blog webpage may provide a solution to that expanding problem.

Facts testify to the acuteness of the issue. In February 2007 the Chinese deliberately but thoughtlessly and ill-advisedly destroyed a satellite of theirs, thereby hugely increasing the amount of space debris (plus 2,500 pieces). That was also a source of worry and embarrassment for them shortly before a Beijing space debris conference. Precisely two years later, two satellites collided, thus adding another 600 pieces. Hardly three years later, a Russian Mars probe was raising concerns as it was set to re-enter the atmosphere and the resulting bits to crash down to earth. But locating that seemed elusive and embarrassed Russians proved unable to give realistic explanations.

Overall close monitoring – NASA's for instance – shows the undeniable rise in space debris – from 10,000 pieces in 2007 to 18,000 in 2009 – including anything from tool-bags to telescopes to disused satellites. The problem lies not in high Earth orbit where the drag is slight but in strong-dragging low orbit where slowed-down objects are likely to fall to Earth or to start an unstoppable chain reaction which is known as the Kessler Syndrome after the pioneer analyst of space debris, who issued warnings as early as 1978. The Chinese incident was feared to have accelerated the reaction likelihood.

Yet all this worrying needs qualifying as so far so good, since there has been no casualty, and anyway debris is being closely tracked. What is more, space is so big that the odds of satellite collisions must be small.

Still the issue needs tackling as, otherwise, launching spacecrafts might become impossible or, at least, increasingly expensive since spacecrafts are bound to require more protection. Could it thus spell the end of space exploration?

Not necessarily actually. As early as 2007 guidelines were issued at the UN level. Conferences are organised round the issue – as in April 2007 in China. Agencies such as NASA, the US Federal Emergency Management Agency and Roscosmos, the Russian space agency, do monitor space. And for instance NASA reportedly designs its satellites so that they cannot re-enter the Earth atmosphere or will fall into oceans. Finally the most recent article refers to a solution which is a Swiss space vacuum cleaner – CleanSpaceOne which is to be launched over the next few years.

Shouldn't further such devices be on the drawing table for space exploration to be sustainable?

500 words

File 4

Health

I. Ready

Documents

- "Childhood obesity battle", adapted from *The New York Times*, 2010
- "Transparent menus to shed pounds", adapted from *The Economist*, 2009
- "One on Two British adults…", adapted from Skynews, 2011
- Cartoon by Jonathan Brown
- Passage from *Harry Potter and the Goblet of Fire*, 2000, J.K. Rowling

Rédiger en anglais et entre 400-500 mots une synthèse des documents proposés. Vous indiquerez avec précision à la fin de votre synthèse le nombre de mots qu'elle comporte. Un écart de 10 % en plus ou en moins sera accepté. Votre synthèse comportera un titre comptabilisé dans le nombre de mots.

Document 1

Childhood obesity battle

February 2010, adapted from *The New York Times*

On Tuesday under the aegis of Michelle Obama, the White House published its widely-encompassing anti-obesity campaign aimed at children and the way they eat and play with new school lunches, playgrounds and even medical visits. Childhood obesity could thus be eradicated within a generation.

This initiative, entitled "Let's Move", marks Mrs Obama's official debut in a high-profile policy role. She has already managed to enlist many partners in government, medicine, science, business, education and athletics. They have all pledged to stop the couch-potatoe tendency amongst children and to have them eat fresher and healthier food.

The same day the three major suppliers of school lunches – Sodexo, Chartwells School Dining Services and Aramark – promised to cut the amounts of fat, sugar and salt in the meals they serve over the next five years. Beverage makers promised more consumer-friendly labeling on all cans, bottles, and vending and fountain machines within two years. The American Academy of Pediatrics called on physicians to measure the body mass Index, an indicator of obesity, in their young patients. Professional athletes from 12 leagues, including football and baseball, have volunteered to promote the message of "60 Minutes of Play a Day" through public service announcements; media companies including the Walt Disney Company and NBC have pledged to broadcast them. [...]

As to Mrs Obama, this is an opportunity for her to turn from her role as mom in chief to one of active public policy promoter during her husband's term in office but that might be politically risky as Republicans denounce the White House as an agent of big government. Mrs Obama should beware of not telling parents off as a food police officer. When complaining about junk food marketing, the First Lady made a few enemies in the food industry. Her campaign may well be controversial. [...]

The White House's initiative was about a year in the making, being discussed with many public health experts. The outcome of the debate for Mrs Obama and her aides was that they should refrain from focusing on the individual behavior of parents and their offspring and instead to reshape the whole nutritional environment of American children – sidewalks should be set up to entice pupils to walk to school, greengrocers should settle in inner cities to make it easier to buy fresh fruit and vegetables. [...]

Childhood obesity rates in the United States have tripled over the past thirty years, and today nearly one in three children in America are overweight or obese. Obesity is blamed by health experts for a variety of medical conditions, among them heart disease, high blood pressure, diabetes, cancer and asthma.

The obesity epidemic might also be damaging to national security, the White House argues – it is now one the most common disqualifiers for military service.

There have already been tentative efforts to fight against childhood obesity in the past but experts say they lacked coordination and some policies were in outright contradiction when, for instance, the Agriculture Department subsidized high fructose corn syrup.

Health experts hailed Tuesday's announcement as a welcome shift. [...]

It will, however, be easier said than done, especially in times of economic crisis when you should count the pennies. And some school lunch providers argue that their efforts to cut fat are being thwarted by some school districts who say such changes are too expensive.

Document 2

Transparent menus to shed pounds

July 2009, adapted from *The Economist*

American restaurants may have to display calories

At the start of this month California started to enforce a new law – it forces 20-branches-and-more-strong chain restaurants to label the items on their menus with calorie counts. California is following in the footsteps of three other states – Oregon, Maine and Massachussets – and 11 city and county governments. The trend has been quick on the uptake, gaining momentum as fast as national waistlines. New York City was the first to pass such a law as early as March 2008. The whole nation is expected to do the same. [...]

More than one American adult out of three are obese and they often find themselves put hard to task when asked to assess the number of calories they consume when they eat out. According to a study in *The American Journal of Public Health* respondents underestimated the calories in unhealthy foods by more than 600 calories, which should account for a bulky 30% of what a woman is supposed to consume on a daily basis.

Those in favour of the menu-labelling law argue that it may entice people to eat healthier foods. For example Los Angeles County's Public Health Department reckons it could prevent almost 40% of the weight gain a year in the county.

However such an outcome is far from being certain and the regulations are too recent for their effects to be properly assessed. Yet that may be irrelevant as some think that anyway consumers have a right to know the calorie-count in a restaurant menu just as clothes labels tell them their components and origins.

Menu labelling may also lead restaurants to offer healthier dishes. In response to New York's menu-labelling law, Cosi, a restaurant chain, created a new menu with healthier items and cut the calorie content of some of its existing sandwiches. As a result, it says, people are switching to the lower-cal products. National chains like Starbucks, McDonald's, Denny's and Dunkin' Donuts have all introduced less calorie-high items since menu labelling went into effect in New York.

These chains, though, say these changes are due to new consumer tastes rather than the law. But worries about having to print supersize calorie counts on their menus may also be held to account.

➡ Document 3

One in two British adults obese by 2030

August 2011, adapted from Skynews

Doctors have warned that almost half of all adults in Britain will be obese by 2030, that is to say totalling some 26 million people then – with another 11 million 20 years from now. They advocate tough government action, including a tax on unhealthy food, so as to slow down the current trend.

Their bleak prediction is part of a series of expert reports commissioned by *The Lancet*.

The doctors have offered a league table of actions – the top of which is a 10% tax on high-calorie food and drinks – that might be taken to curb the epidemic.

Professor Klim McPherson, an epidemiologist at Oxford University, said the government needs to learn the lesson of tobacco taxation, which has dramatically reduced smoking rates.

"A tax wouldn't be unpopular if people knew what the issues are," he told Sky News. "People know obesity is a real problem. People don't know, as individuals, what to do about it. Governments do know what to do about it and if they could persuade people, as they easily could, it would be a popular action."

The other suggestions include restricting junk food advertising and warning children to get off the couch and refrain from sitting around watching TV.

The experts assert such initiatives are much more cost-effective than obesity surgery and fat drugs.

Tam Fry, of the National Obesity Forum, said: "Children are born thin. It's what we do to children that makes them obese. Adults have choice, but children can't make informed decisions about what they're eating."

A spokesman for The Department of Health said obesity was a priority. "We are encouraging people to make simple changes, such as eating more fruit and vegetables, cutting down on fatty foods and being more active. We have no current plans to impose a 'fat tax', but we are working with food companies to reduce fat, sugar and salt and ensure healthier options are available."

Document 4

A cartoon by Jonathan Brown

Document 5

Harry Potter and the Goblet of Fire

J.K. Rowling, 2000

Uncle Vernon and Aunt Petunia had managed to find excuses for [their son's] bad marks as usual [...]. However, at the bottom of the report there were a few well chosen comments from the school nurse which not even Uncle Vernon and Aunt Petunia could explain away. No matter how much Aunt Petunia wailed that Dudley was big-boned, and that his poundage was really puppy-fat, and that he was a growing boy who needed plenty of food, the fact remained that the school outfitters didn't stock knickerbockers big enough for him any more. The school nurse had seen what Aunt Petunia's eyes – so sharp when it came to spotting fingerprints on her gleaming walls, and in observing the comings and goings of the neighbours – simply refused to see: that, far from needing extra nourishment, Dudley had reached roughly the size and weight of a young killer whale.

So – after many tantrums, after arguments that shook Harry's bedroom floor, and many tears from Aunt Petunia – the new regime had begun. The diet sheet had been taped to the fridge, which had been emptied of all Dudley's favourite things – fizzy drinks and cakes, chocolate bars and burgers – and filled instead with fruit and vegetables and the sorts of things that Uncle Vernon called "rabbit food".

2. Steady

a. Tableau de synthèse

Cf. page suivante.

b. Theme: health, obesity

- **Question:** Can anti-obesity measures be effective?
- **Outline:**
  I. Situations in the US & UK
  II. Measures about sport/exercise
  III. Measures about food

Childhood obesity battle *The New York Times*, Feb. 2010	Transparent menus to shed pounds *The Economist*, July 2009	One in two British adults will be obese… *Skynews*, Aug 2011	Cartoon, Jonathan Brown	*Harry Potter and the Goblet of Fire* J.K. Rowling
US	US	UK	US	UK
Let's Move campaign to eliminate childhood obesity, led by Michelle Obama	New calorie-labelling laws	Prediction of rise in adults obesity, from 15 to 26 m, i.e. 1/2	Useless ban on sodas in schools	Blindness of some parents to their child's weight Unawareness
<u>Facts</u>: 1/3 children obese; x 3 in 30 years; consequently medical conditions & impact on security as obese people are unfit for army; past efforts thwarted by some economic subsidies <u>Partners</u>: federal government, doctors, scientists, firms, schools & athletes <u>Actions</u>: providing healthier lunches, better labelling on snacks & cans, measuring BMIs, recording awareness raising messages & broadcasting them, installing sidewalks & greengrocers <u>Risks</u>: for M. Obama not to become a food police agent of big government; opposition of the food industry <u>Advice</u>: not to focus on individuals but on their surroundings <u>Impediments</u>: current tight school budgets, hence reluctance to implement measures	<u>Fact</u>: > 1/3 US people obese & unable to assess calories in restaurant food <u>Goals</u>: entice people to opt for healthier food & prevent weight gain <u>Opposition</u>: doubtful efficacy Counter-argument: right to know <u>Result</u>: restaurants alter their menus with healthier choices though claim an answer to clients' demand	<u>Facts</u>: 15 m obese people & they know it's a problem <u>Argument</u>: children are victims <u>Measures</u>: a) taxes on high calorie food / / tobacco taxes; b) limiting junk food ads; c) campaign to make kids exercise <u>Partners</u>: food industry to offer healthier food <u>Goal</u>: encouraging people to eat healthily & exercise	<u>Risks</u>: Need to explain Denouncing nanny state & infantilising	<u>Risks</u>: junk food vs rabbit food (extreme diets)

3. Go

Tackling obesity

Obesity has become a soaring real scourge in the USA and in the UK, where both local and national governments and experts have taken, or are suggesting, measures to tackle the epidemic. These suggestions are the focus of a 2010 *New York Times* article, a 2009 *Economist* article and a cartoon dealing with US obesity, and a 2011 Skynews webpage and an excerpt from J.K.Rowling's *Harry Potter* for the UK. They not only highlight the extent of the trend but more especially put forward exercise promotion on the one hand and food-related anti-obesity measures on the other. Can they be effective?

In the UK, the rate of obesity is very likely to reach 50% among adults by 2030 while currently a third of Americans are obese, including one child in three, the latter figure having tripled in 30 years. This takes a toll on people's health but also on national security as those obese cannot serve in the army. People and especially parents are not necessarily aware of the problem as Rowling implicitly points it out while children can be seen as helpless victims, being also unaware as shown by the cartoon. British doctors want the government to act while both the White House-especially Mrs Obama-and local governments are at the forefront of anti-obesity campaigns.

One root of the epidemic is the lack of exercise. The authorities should set up campaigns to make kids exercise. For instance, Mrs Obama's "Let's Move" initiative aims to make it easier by improving people's surroundings with sidewalks for instance and to raise their awareness with messages recorded by athletes and broadcast by leading media – *The New York Times* reports. That is thought to work.

Yet the other root, namely bad diets, is rather more widely targeted. In 2009 – *The Economist* reports – more and more US local authorities were forcing eateries to calorie-label their menus. Likewise Mrs Obama wishes for better labelling on snacks and sodas which might also be even banned-on the cartoon. Yet these nannying measures are questioned, being possibly useless and proof of impinging big government's action. Restaurants claim they have anyhow changed their menus owing to changing tastes, reinforcing the idea of labelling pointlessness. As to schools which should provide healthier lunches and advice, they might be reluctant to do so due to tight budgets. Money could be the key – that is what experts say, like for tobacco – with taxes on high-calorie food in the UK. Such food should also stopped being extensively advertised. Yet getting rid of it entirely to favour "rabbit" food might be questioned too-as in *Harry Potter*. Anyhow that requires having places to buy such food-hence Mrs Obama's wish to see more greengrocers. Finally the food industry might show its opposition, especially in the US given that it had formerly been subsidised there.

Some governmental partners in anti-obesity campaigns therefore might well put a spanner in the works.

485 words

File 5

Technologies & privacy

I. Ready

Documents

- "Technology at loggerheads with privacy", adapted from *The Guardian*, August 2010
- "Protecting private data in the global panopticon", adapted from *The Economist*, December 1999
- "Beware of online investigations", adapted from *The Guardian*, November 2007
- "Saving fuel by being spied upon", adapted from *The Economist*, September 2010
- Passage from *The Terrible Privacy of Maxwell Sim*, Jonathan Coe, 2010

Rédiger en anglais et en 400 mots une synthèse des documents proposés. Vous indiquerez avec précision à la fin de votre synthèse le nombre de mots qu'elle comporte. Un écart de 10 % en plus ou en moins sera accepté. Votre synthèse comportera un titre comptabilisé dans le nombre de mots.

Document 1

Technology at loggerheads with privacy

Adapted from *The Guardian*, August 2010

Do you have a boy/girl-friend? What is your religion? Which political party do you support? What did you do last night? The answers to those personal questions which used to be given only to the happy few we know and trust are now voluntarily posted online.

The boundaries of what should be publicly revealed and unveiled are getting more and more blurred what with Big-Brother-like TV shows and widespread CCTVs. Yet social network websites are what really challenges the most the notion of privacy – some 500 million people are sharing their lives on Facebook now.

"We're seeing new concerns starting to emerge around the issue of privacy," says Stephen Balkam, a member of Facebook's safety advisory board. "The battle lines are being drawn between generations. Facebook is headed by someone who hasn't hit 30 yet, and who has very different perceptions about what is private and what is not. We need to recognise that with social networking, geolocation and digital technology, the privacy bar is being reset."

As technology companies gain momentum, now cultural and ethical challenges spring up. A case in point is that of Google's StreetView which has been repeatedly attacked by privacy advocates and lobbies who question whether the benefits of making every property in every street visible on the web are worth the sacrifice of the individual's right to privacy.

What can account for Facebook's success? its requiring to have people's real identities whereas formerly on internet people used to use pseudonyms. From anonymity to publicity, the internet has moved on to a new phase, curbing the trend in which faceless, nameless commentators could easily post abusive messages.

But if this new internet world makes you jittery, do not try to think too hard about the future. We are already bombarded by pinpointed adverts based on our Google inquiries, or are picked out by our age and interests on Facebook, and the future will be even more personalised. "Sites will get much better at predicting our behaviour, serving us what we feel like buying and finding new ways to share information," says a researcher.

➠ Document 2

Protecting private data in the global panopticon

Adapted from *The Economist*, December 1999

Today the information economy poses a powerful challenge to privacy with the proliferation of databases and internet use. Consumer defense groups and privacy proponents are calling for more efficient protection laws while companies manage to deftly and cunningly pay lip-service to the respect of their customers' privacy. People's wish to retain some form of control over who knows what about them rubs against new service companies' need to get and use that very information. Without their growing databases, firms would not be able to tailor their products to individual tastes, handle secure electronic transactions, offer streamlined payment and delivery, or target their advertising and promotion.

The United States and the European Union are locked in a potentially damaging trade dispute over how to find the right balance between privacy and the demands of trading businesses. The 1995 EU Data Protection Directive is one of the most stringent and nearly-all-encompassing privacy laws in today's world. All EU members are committed to implementing it domestically although few have done so so far. Some already have quite strict laws on their books. American companies consider the EU directives as draconian and unworkable, and object to the huge barrier to the transatlantic transmission of information. Washington wants the EU to follow in its own footsteps and accept self-regulation which is thought by Americans to suffice to protect data exchanges.

Is all this fuss about privacy justified? Has new technology really made it easier than in the past to dig up information about someone? In one sense, it has. [...] Once dozens, even hundreds, of individual telephone books would have had to be consulted to complete a search which now takes seconds. [...] Is the growing band of privacy campaigners right that we should be alarmed?

➡ Document 3

Beware of online investigations

Adapted from *The Guardian*, November 2007

When looking for information on job applicants on social network websites, firms could well be infringing on privacy, an internet expert has said.

John Carr, chairman of the UK Coalition on Internet Safety, thinks that employers and education officials could be crossing a Rubicon when they dig up information about applicants on the web.

"There are lots of rumours about young job applicants being screened on Google or even university tutors looking at people applying for higher education," he said.

"If that really is happening, then it could be illegal – when the kids are posting a picture of a party, they are only doing it to let their mates look. They are not doing it for an application form."

In Britain, although there are data protection laws to stop private information from being sneakily picked up by third parties, regulators say that the internet area is a moot point – getting access to information which is publicly available on the web may not be illegal; and it is up to individuals to protect their information online.

"Essentially, if an individual looked at someone else's profile on a social networking site, it would not be a breach of data protection," said a spokeswoman for the ICO, Britain's privacy watchdog.

However, it remains unclear whether organisations covertly accessing people's private web pages or email accounts would constitute a breach of the law. Last week the ICO issued guidelines, urging users of social networking sites such as Facebook and Bebo to take their privacy more seriously.

Document 4

Saving fuel by being spied upon

Adapted from *The Economist*, September 2010

Should you wish to drive more economically there is now a whole range of new devices to help you. And if you run a car or truck company you are bound to jump for such fuel-saving "eco-assist" systems. Internet devices might even enable you to get more information abour your drivers' behaviour.

One such device is used by Masternaut Three X, a British company that specialises in vehicle tracking. It taps into the engine-management system which, because of the increasing amount of electronics used in cars, contains data that can be analysed to monitor such things as excessive revving and harsh braking. Drivers can then get warnings on their dashboards. Firms using such systems say they can yield fuel savings of around 10% a year.

Not only does it make it possible to discover those with the heaviest feet on the accelerator pedal who could do with retraining, this can also help reduce accidents. […]

Greenroad, a Californian driver-monitoring company, does not need to tap into the car's computer. It uses GPS to measure the speed of a vehicle and a set of accelerometers to measure the forces acting on the car as it accelerates, brakes and turns. The data are used to determine how the vehicle is being driven and the results are shown to the driver as green, amber or red LEDs. For fleet cars, the data can also be sent to a control centre, so that Big Brother can tick off offending drivers.

Some claim that despite the Orwellian overtones most drivers will soon become comfortable with the device and value the fuel savings it offers. […]

Document 5

The Terrible Privacy of Maxwell Sim

Jonathan Coe, 2010, ch. 12

When I pressed the button, anyway, a map appeared. It showed the motorway I was driving on, and it showed me – or at least my car – as a little red arrow heading determinedly forward in an eastbound direction. How many satellites were trained on me at that moment, I wondered, in order to calculate this ever-changing position? I'd read somewhere that it was always about five: five pairs of eyes keeping me under constant surveillance, from their vantage point high up in the sky. Was this a reassuring thought, or a frightening one? As usual, I couldn't quite decide.

2. Steady

a. Tableau de synthèse

Cf. page suivante.

b. Theme: new technologies & privacy

- **Question:** Do technological advances infringe on privacy?
- **Outline:**
    1. Technologies
    2. Economic/business view
    3. Legal perspective
    4. Ethical perspective

Technology at loggerheads…, Aug 2010, *The Guardian*	**Protecting private data…, Dec 1999, *The Economist***	**Beware of online investigations, Nov 2007, *The Guardian***	**Gently does it. Motoring, Sep 2010, *The Economist***	***Maxwell Sim*, Jonathan Coe, 2012**
<u>Facts</u>: • More & more people put more & more info online esp. on social networks • Generation gap: social networkers under-30 with a lower privacy bar than their elder • Facebook, a new Internet stage, from anonymity to real identity online <u>Sources of monitoring</u>: Big Brother entertainment show, CCTV, geolocation, digital technology, social networks, Google's StreetView <u>Wrangling & fears</u>: questioning over StreetView; future bound to go further in privacy invasion as websites monitor & use users' data so as to do their business	Privacy vs business/eco Information companies – esp. on Internet – feed on the private data individuals reveal while yearning for some privacy control US vs EU dispute over data exchanges • US & self-regulation • EU a strict privacy protecting law It's truly easier to quickly find info about other people but is it alarming?	A warning: <u>Source</u>: UK Coalition on Internet Safety <u>Statement</u>: searching info about education & job applicants on social networks = privacy breach <u>Reaction</u>: GB protection laws exist but up to individuals to protect their data online, that is publicly available + ICO, GB privacy watchdog, issued guidance to urge users to be careful	Vehicle-tracking & monitoring via electronic systems onboard &/ or GPS <u>Goals</u>: • Cut fuel consumption • Reduce accidents • Fining offenders <u>Companies</u>: • GB Masternaut Three X • US Green Road Fear: Orwellian side	GPS monitoring, surveillance. → should you care?

Orwellian Technologies?

There is growing concern over information technologies that monitor people. Do these technological advances infringe on privacy? That is the question raised by a 2010 *Guardian* article, a 1999 *Economist* business-and-law-focusing paper, a 2007 *Guardian* British-oriented column, a 2010 *Economist* monitoring-based article and an excerpt from one of Jonathan Coe's novels, which highlight features of the problem.

These technologies first need defining. They include Internet and especially social networks but also means of geolocation such as GPS as well as digital electronics, entertainment shows and information firms as Google. All of them basically have access to their users' accounts or deeds and behaviours.

And this is actually the very backbone and engine of their businesses. Information companies thrive on the information users give about themselves. Likewise firms as British Masternaut Three X and American Greenroad base their operations on vehicle-tracking via electronic systems onboard and/or GPS so as to help motor companies to cut fuel consumption while reducing accidents, or simply drivers to find their way. International data exchanges as those between the US and the EU are also at stake.

Here comes the rub of legal wrangling. As reported in 1999, the US favours self-regulation while the EU is for stricter privacy protecting rules. But within a country as Britain, there are protection laws – though privacy watchdogs warn that may not be enough when it comes to recruiting universities and companies delving into social network accounts to retrieve information about applicants. The official answer is that users should be careful and that it is up to them to protect their data as they have been told to do.

Actually *the Guardian* reminds that the younger users are, the more likely they are to put more and more accurate private information. Facebook testifies to the fact that the limits to privacy tend to get flimsier for the under-30-year-olds such as its founder. That is why finding information about other people is also getting easier and easier. Some companies might even take action as fining offending drivers. There is definitely an Orwellian side to all this surveillance but do or should people care about it? Coe's narrator does not know but watchdogs do worry and so do the newspapers of the file and implicitly the British author.

Information technology users, beware!

385 words

File 6

9/11

Centrale 2012
(MP, PC, PSI)

I. Ready

CONCOURS CENTRALE•SUPÉLEC

Anglais

MP, PC, PSI

4 heures — Calculatrices interdites

2012

L'usage de tout système électronique ou informatique est interdit dans cette épreuve.

Rédiger en anglais et en 500 mots environ une synthèse des documents proposés. Vous indiquerez avec précision à la fin de votre synthèse le nombre de mots qu'elle comporte. Un écart de 10% en plus ou en moins sera accepté. Votre travail comportera un titre comptabilisé dans le nombre de mots.

Ce sujet propose les 3 documents suivants :

1. « Day's End », article paru le 27 août 2011 dans le *New York Magazine*, accompagné de deux photographies;
2. la critique du livre « The Submission », parue dans le *International Herald Tribune* du 17 août 2011;
3. un extrait du roman « Extremely Loud and Incredibly Close » de Jonathan Safran Foer, publié en 2005.

L'ordre dans lequel se présentent les documents est aléatoire.

New York
NEWS & FEATURES

Day's End

The 9/11 decade is now over. The terrorists lost. But who won?

by Franck Rich — Aug 27, 2011

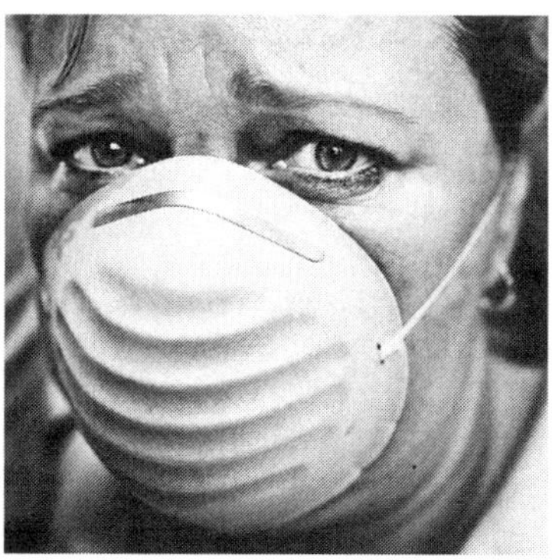

Mid-September 2001
(Photo: Peter Funch)

August 5, 2011
(Photo: Benjamin Norman/The New York Times/Redux)

[...]

Three red-letter days in 2011 have certified the passing of the 9/11 decade as we had known it. The first, of course, was the killing of Osama bin Laden. We demand that our stories have beginnings, middles, and ends. While bin Laden's demise wasn't the final curtain for radical-Islamic terrorism, it was a satisfying resolution of the classic "dead or alive" Western that George W. Bush had dangled so tantalizingly before the nation in 2001, only to let the bad guy get away at Tora Bora. Once bin Laden was gone, he was gone from our politics, too. Terrorism has disappeared as a campaign issue; the old Bush-Cheney fear card can't be found in the playbook of the GOP presidential contenders. Ron Paul's isolationism increasingly seems like his party's mainstream while the neocon orthodoxy of McCain-Palin looks like the cranky fringe.

The other red-letter days were August 5 and 6, with their twin calamities: the downgrading of America by Standard & Poor's and the downing of a Chinook helicopter by the Taliban, making for the single most fatal day for Americans in Afghanistan. Among the fallen in that bloodbath were 17 Navy Seals, some of them members of the same revered team that had vanquished bin Laden[1]. Yet their tragic deaths were runners-up in national attention next to our fiscal woes. America may still ostensibly be a country at war with terrorists, but that war is at most a low-grade fever for the vast American majority with no direct connection to the men and women fighting it. The battle consuming our attention and our energies these days is the losing struggle to stay financially afloat. In time, the connection between the ten-year-old war in Afghanistan and our new civil war over America's three-year-old economic crisis may well prove the most consequential historical fact of the hideous decade they bracket.

THE hallowed burial grounds of 9/11 were supposed to bequeath us a stronger nation, not a busted one. We were supposed to be left with a finer legacy than Gitmo and the Patriot Act. When we woke up on September 12, we imagined a whole host of civic virtues that might rise from the smoldering ruins. The New Normal promised a new national unity and, of all unlikely miracles, bi-partisanship: The still-green president had a near-perfect approval rating for weeks. We would at last cast off our two-decade holiday from history, during which we had mostly ignored a steady barrage of terrorist threats and attacks. We would embrace a selfless wartime patriotism built on the awesome example of those regular Americans who ran to the rescue on that terrifying day of mass death, at the price of their own health and sometimes their lives.

What arrived instead, sadly enough, was another hijacking—of 9/11 by those who exploited it for motives large and petty, both ideological and crassly commercial. The most lethal of these hijackings was the Bush administration's repurposing of 9/11 for a war against a country that had not attacked us. So devilishly clever was the selling of the Saddam-for-Osama bait-and-switch that almost half the country would come to believe that Iraqis were among the 9/11 hijackers. No less shabby, if far less catastrophic, was the milking of 9/11 for the lesser causes of self-promotion and product placement by those seeking either power or profit. From the Bush-reelection campaign ad with an image of a flag-draped stretcher carrying remains at ground zero to the donning of flag pins by television anchors and pandering politicians, no opportunistic appropriation of 9/11 was too sleazy to be off-limits.

[...]

IN retrospect, the most consequential event of the past ten years may not have been 9/11 or the Iraq War but the looting of the American economy by those in power in Washington and on Wall Street. This was happening in plain sight—or so we can now see from a distance. At the time, we were so caught up in Al Qaeda's external threat to America that we didn't pay proper attention to the more prosaic threats within.

In such an alternative telling of the decade's history, the key move Bush made after 9/11 had nothing to do with military strategy or national-security policy. It was instead his considered decision to rule out shared sacrifice as a governing principle for the fight ahead. Sacrifice was high among the unifying ideals that many Americans hoped would emerge from the rubble of ground zero, where so many Good Samaritans had practiced it. But the president scuttled the notion on the first weekend after the attack, telling Americans that it was his "hope" that "they make no sacrifice whatsoever" beyond, perhaps, tolerating enhanced airline security. Few leaders in either party contradicted him. Bush would soon implore us to "get down to Disney World in Florida" and would even lend his image to a travel-industry ad promoting tourism. Our marching orders were to go shopping.

From then on, it was a given that any human losses at wartime would be borne by a largely out-of-sight, out-of-mind, underpaid volunteer army and that the expense would be run up on a magic credit card. Even as the rising insurgency in Iraq began to stress American resources to the max in 2003, Bush doubled down on new tax cuts and pushed through a wildly extravagant new Medicare entitlement for prescription drugs to shore up his reelection prospects with elderly voters. David Walker, then the comptroller general, called it "the most reckless fiscal year in the history of the republic." But Americans took the money and ran, and the same partisan voices now screaming about deficits in Washington remained mum as the cascade of red ink soared into the multitrillions.

By portraying Afghanistan and Iraq as utterly cost-free to a credulous public, the Bush administration injected the cancer into the American body politic that threatens it today: If we don't need new taxes to fight two wars, why do we need them for anything? But that's only half the story in this alternative chronicle of the decade's history. Even as the middle class was promised a free ride, those at the top were awarded a free pass—not just with historically low tax rates that compounded America's rampant economic inequality but with lax supervision of their own fiscal misbehavior.

It was only a month after 9/11 that the Enron scandal erupted, kicking off a larger narrative that would persist for the rest of the decade. The Houston energy company was a corporate Ponzi scheme that anticipated the antics at financial institutions, mortgage mills, and credit-rating agencies during the subprime scam. Enron had also been the biggest patron of Bush's political career, and so the president dutifully promised a crackdown, with a new "financial crimes SWAT team" and "tough new criminal penalties for corporate fraud." But this propaganda campaign was no more reality-based than the one that would promote Saddam's weapons of mass destruction. Once the Enron collapse became old news, federal regulatory agencies and law enforcement were encouraged to go fishing as the housing bubble inflated and banks manufactured toxic paper that would send America and the world into a ruinous dive rivaling bin Laden's cruelest fantasies.

It is that America—the country where rampaging greed usurped the common good in wartime, the country that crashed just as Bush fled the White

House—that we live in today. It has little or no resemblance to the generous and heroic America we glimpsed on 9/11 and the days that followed. Our economy and our politics are broken. We remain in hock to jihadist oil producers as well as to China. Our longest war stretches into an infinite horizon. After watching huge expenditures of American blood and treasure install an Iran-allied "democracy" in a still-fratricidal Iraq, Americans have understandably resumed their holiday from history where it left off, turning their backs on the Arab Spring.

Thanks to the killing of the mastermind of the 9/11 attacks and the scattering of Al Qaeda, at least no one can say, ten years later, that the terrorists won. But if there's anything certain about the new decade ahead, it's that sooner or later we will have to address the question of exactly who did.

This article has been corrected to show that 17 Navy Seals were killed by the downing of the Chinook helicopter in Afghanistan, not 22.

International Herald Tribune
THE GLOBAL EDITION OF THE NEW YORK TIMES

August 17, 2011

Wrestling with America's post-9/11 traumas

The Submission. By Amy Waldman. 299 pages. *Farrar, Straus & Giroux*, $26; *William Heinemann*, £12.99

BY MICHIKO KAKUTANI

[...]

Ms. Waldman, a former reporter for The New York Times, imagines what would happen if a jury in charge of selecting a ground zero-like memorial were to choose, from among the many anonymous submissions, a design that turns out to have been created by a Muslim-American architect.

Though this may sound, in summary, like a contrived, high-concept premise, Ms. Waldman not only captures the political furor and media storm that ensue, but also gives us an intimate, immediate sense of the fallout that these events have on the individuals involved. They include: Mohammad Khan (or "Mo," as he's known to family and friends), the architect whose winning design brings him notoriety and condemnation instead of praise; Claire Burwell, a wealthy widow and the families' representative on the jury, whose early championing of Mo's design later gives way to nagging doubts; Paul Rubin, the jury's pragmatic chairman, who's eager to find a politically viable solution to the whole situation; Sean Gallagher, a protester, whose brother died in the attacks; and Asma Anwar, an illegal Bangladeshi immigrant whose husband was also a victim.

Writing in limber, detailed prose, Ms. Waldman has created a choral novel with a big historical backdrop and pointillist emotional detail, a novel that gives the reader a visceral understanding of how New York City and the country at large reacted to 9/11, and how that terrible day affected some Americans' attitudes toward Muslims and immigrants.

[...] In these pages she charts how one decision or choice can turn into a billiard ball, ricocheting at unexpected angles and creating chain reactions — especially when it's been put in play in a tinderbox of ethnic, religious and regional politics, and its impact has been magnified and distorted by the echo chamber of 24/7 news media coverage.

In this case the precipitating event is the jury's choice of a memorial design referred to as "the Garden," a rectangular space, divided by perpendicular canals, planted with real trees and steel ones (made from salvaged scraps of the original buildings brought down by the terrorists) and surrounded by a "white perimeter wall," on whose interior the victims' names would be listed. Claire lobbies for the Garden, despite objections from other jury members that it is "too beautiful," too sentimental, too obviously a symbol of healing. The rest of the jury eventually comes around to support her choice, partly because of her impassioned arguments, partly because of the emotional authority she embodies as the families' representative.

When word leaks that the winning choice was designed by a Muslim, a nationwide uproar follows, reminiscent of the real-life one last year over plans to build a mosque near ground zero. The jury is dismissed as a bunch of elitist Manhattan artists, oblivious to the nation's feelings. The leader of a group named Save America From Islam calls the garden a "martyrs' paradise" that's been smuggled into the memorial like a Trojan horse. Muslim women are assaulted, their headscarves pulled off in random attacks, and mosques are desecrated around the country.

As for Mo, he suddenly finds himself "analyzed, judged and invented" by strangers. Raised in Alexandria, Virginia, by parents who emigrated from India in 1966, Mo had "barely been to a mosque in his life." His parents "made modernity their religion," and Mo was, "if not an atheist himself, certainly agnostic, which perhaps made him not a Muslim at all."

A graduate of the Yale School of Art and Architecture and a member of a prestigious architectural firm, Mo is a talented yuppie with all-American dreams of success. When the jury waffles on its selection of his design, and it is suggested that he either withdraw or somehow alter it, he grows indignant and increasingly angry. Death threats, pickets and photographers force him to leave his apartment, while denunciations from imams — who accuse him of blasphemy — rain down upon him as well.

The pretentious intellectual squabbles over the choice of the memorial; the cynical attempts by politicians to position themselves on the debate; the tactical maneuverings of special-interest groups; the cascade of inflammatory commentary from pundits on the right and left; and the speculation, lies and rumors fueled by the Internet — all are deftly conjured by Ms. Waldman.

Ms. Waldman tends to favor sympathy over satire when it comes to limning her characters' feelings and motivations, with the notable exception of the fictional New York Post reporter Alyssa Spier, who is portrayed in over-the-top terms as a mercenary tabloid hussy, willing to distort and sensationalize the facts in order to promote her own career. Alyssa asserts that "the problem with Islam is Islam," and goes out of her way to avoid being fair and balanced, including trying to influence Claire's attitude toward Mo.

Although the evolution of Claire's thinking about the memorial may not make that much sense to the reader — this and the cartoony portrait of Alyssa are the novel's two big flaws — Ms. Waldman does an affecting job of showing how people who have lost relatives in the terrorist attack are trying to grapple with their own confusion and conflicting emotions, even as they find themselves caught up in a political conflagration. Indeed, it is Ms. Waldman's ability to depict their grief and anger that lends this novel its extraordinary emotional ballast, and that reminds us how inextricably linked the personal and the political, the private and the public have become in our post-9/11 world.

(The narrator is a nine-year old boy whose father was killed in the World Trade Center terrorist attack on September 11, 2001.)

When Mom tucked me in that night, she could tell that something was on my mind, and asked if I wanted to talk. I did, but not to her, so I said, "No offense, but no." "Are you sure?" "*Très fatigué,*" I said, waving my hand. "Do you want me to read something to you?" "It's OK." "We could go through the *New York Times* for mistakes." "No, thank you." "All right," she said, "all right." She gave me a kiss and turned off the light, and then, as she was about to go, I said, "Mom?" and she said, "Yes?" and I said, "Do you promise not to bury me when I die?"

She came back over and put her hand on my cheek and said, "You're not going to die." I told her, "I am." She said, "You're not going to die any time soon. You have a long, long life ahead of you." I told her, "As you know, I'm extremely brave, but I can't spend eternity in a small underground place. I just can't. Do you love me?" "Of course I love you." "Then put me in one of those mausoleum-thingies." "A mausoleum?" "Like I read about." "Do we have to talk about this?" "Yes." "Now?" "Yes." "Why?" "Because what if I die tomorrow?" "You're not going to die tomorrow." "Dad didn't think he was going to die the next day." "That's not going to happen to you." "It wasn't going to happen to him." "Oskar." "I'm sorry, but I just can't be buried." "Don't you want to be with Dad and me?" "Dad isn't even there!" "Excuse me?" "His body was destroyed." "Don't talk like that." "Talk like what? It's the truth. I don't understand why everyone pretends he's there." "Take it easy Oskar." "It's just an empty box." "It's more than an empty box." "Why would I want to spend eternity next to an empty box?"

Mom said, "His spirit is there," and that made me *really* angry. I told her, "Dad didn't have a spirit! He had cells!" "His memory is there." "His memory is here," I said pointing at my head.

Jonathan Safran Foer, *Extremely Loud and Incredibly Close*
New York: Penguin, 2005, p. 168.

2. Steady

a. Tableau de synthèse

Cf. page suivante.

b. Theme: 9/11

- **Question:** How can the 9/11 aftermath be assessed?
- **Outline:**
  I. On an individual scale
  II. On a national scale

Day's End ***New York Magazine*,** **27 Aug. 2011**	**Photo** **Mid-Sept. 2001**	**Photo** **Aug. 5, 2011**	**Wrestling with America's post-9/11 traumas** ***International Herald Tribune*,** **17 Aug. 2011**	***Extremely Loud and Incredibly Close*** **Jonathan S. Foer, 2005**
Political & economic approaches to 9/11 legacy 10 years later Indictment of today's US greed vs 9/11 heroic generosity & withdrawal from world affairs (e.g. Arab spring & Iraq)	Human grief at 9/11	S&P's down-grading US Financial grief	Book review: *The Submission*, by Amy Waldman 9/11 consequences on the US & US attitudes to Muslims	Literary excerpt
<u>2011 facts:</u> Bin Laden's killing; S&P's US downgrading; US helicopter shot down by Talibans → 17 casualties <u>Contrast</u>: terrorism < economic crisis <u>Assessment of the decade</u>: post 9/11 hopes (unity, international involvement, civility, selfless patriotism) shattered & replaced or distorted by Afghan war, Iraq invasion & political & economic interests Blaming: criminal profit-seekers (top politicians & traders) superseding 9/11 a) Bush bec. "ruled out sacrifice as a governing principle" although post 9/11 cause for unity b) & adopted a capitalist money-making consumerist approach c) & fought terrorism only abroad though expensive, hence wild budget making, leading to debt-ridden US (a muted side) d) "mad" economic decisions: tax cuts, ↑ Medicare, low tax rates, lax fiscal monitoring of the wealthiest – the Oct2001 Enron scandal was a forerunner of a 3-year-old crisis with no real sanctions despite promises (political manoeuvring) e) Withdrawal from word affairs, e.g. Arab Spring Who won the post 9/11 fight?			Post 9/11 fiction about Ground Zero plans Muslim architect's design chosen but media & political uproar <u>Relatives' reaction</u>: sensitivity, emotions, confusion, grief, anger <u>Political reactions</u>: cynicism, violence or being finicky, xenophobia, anti-Muslim attacks <u>Media reaction</u>: 21/7 monitoring by tabloids, grim portrayal <u>Overall reaction</u>: fierce, against design & designer because a Muslim although not practicing – he's attacked by all sides Condemnation of intellectual squabbles over the choice of design	9/11 victims' relatives' trauma, esp. children. Problem of no corpse What is death? Memories in the mind > Ground Zero memorial

Assessing the aftermath of 9/11

9/11 and more specifically its tenth anniversary triggered many comments and memories as well as literary output, all meaning to take a step back to make in-depth assessments. Franck Rich's *New York Magazine* Bush-indicting article and accompanying photos together with the *International Herald Tribune* review on The Submission by Amy Waldman and an excerpt from Jonathan S. Foer's novel beg the question of how the aftermath of 9/11 can be assessed on both an individual and a national scale.

The September 2001 photo bears witness as to the horror and grief entailed by 9/11; and so do the books of fiction afore-mentioned. Emotions ran high both at the time and they still do a decade later. Relatives – as Foer's young narrator and Waldman's characters – find it very hard to overcome their sorrow and accept the commemoration plans; so much so that they must voice their anger and confusion. Can emotions and memories better find home in an all-too-obviously peaceful memorial or in one's head? Waldman condemns the intellectual fuss over Ground Zero while Foer shows how enduring and mind-embedded memories can be.

Americans heroically rose to the occasion, willing to make sacrifices, embodying key virtues of united citizenship, reminds Rich who, however, deems that the hopes that were thus raised were shattered by selfish profiteering politicians, and also by sensation-seeking 21/7 media in Waldman's view. For instance anti-Muslim feelings began being vented as a result while citizens were talked into being mere consumers.

So which arguments can be given for such fierce judgments? What were the consequences of 9/11 nationwide?

Tackling the site of the attack led to an uproar which is fictitiously re-written by Waldman who points out the new anti-Muslim attacks with her Muslim memorial designer bearing the brunt of it from all sides. Yet she also denounces, like Rich, the behaviour of politicians: finicky, xenophobic, manoeuvring.

Nonetheless, Rich goes further, pinpointedly blaming Bush for his disastrous ill-thought-out and selfish economic and foreign policies. Ten years later terrorism – fought only abroad – is defeated (bin Laden has been killed) and no longer at the forefront. But the Afghanistan and Iraq wars turned out to be so expensive that wild budgets were made, further indebting the US while entailing further terrible casualties – as with a helicopter shot down by the Talibans. Actually Rich puts the onus on politically-engineered American greed for the US renewed withdrawal from world affairs – Arab Spring ignored – and economic crisis. Foolish taxation and spending decisions, though unacknowledged, subsidised those foreign wars and made the US utterly debt-ridden. The barely punished October 2001 Enron scandal was a forerunner of a 3-year-old crisis by 2011, a crisis epitomized by traders' dismay at the US being downgraded by S&P (photo taken on August 5, 2011). That is why Rich thinks the current appalling economic situation is the real and paramount consequence of 9/11 and its follow-up.

History could have been misunderstood. A decade after 9/11, though terrorism has faded, memories and shattered ideals as well as politics and the economy clearly endure.

511 words

File 7

The death penalty

Centrale 2012 (TSI)

I. Ready

CONCOURS CENTRALE•SUPÉLEC

Anglais

TSI **2012**

4 heures Calculatrices interdites

L'usage de tout système électronique ou informatique est interdit dans cette épreuve.

Rédigez en anglais et en 500 mots environ une synthèse des documents proposés. Vous indiquerez avec précision à la fin de votre synthèse le nombre de mots qu'elle comporte. Un écart de 10% en plus ou en moins sera accepté. Votre travail comportera un titre comptabilisé dans le nombre de mots.

Ce sujet propose les 4 documents suivants :

1. un article du *Guardian Weekly* paru le 30 septembre 2011 ;
2. un article paru dans *The Economist* le 24 septembre 2011 ;
3. un dessin de presse de Clay Bennett publié dans le « Chattanooga Times Free Press » du 21 septembre 2011 ;
4. les résultats de sondages d'opinion réalisés aux États-Unis par l'institut Gallup.

L'ordre dans lequel se présentent les documents est aléatoire.

Execution fuels row over death penalty

Opponents say case of Troy Davis is a wake-up call to US politicians

Ed Pilkington Jackson, Georgia

In statistical terms, it may have been just another execution. But, on the morning after the death by lethal injection of Troy Davis, there was no sign that the controversy over the case would be buried with him.

Davis was sent to his death despite a mass of evidence that left his 1991 conviction in doubt, including recantations from seven of the nine key witnesses at his trial for the murder of a police officer.

The execution has provoked an extraordinary outpouring of protest in Georgia, at the supreme court and White House in Washington, and in cities around the world. Relatives of Davis and civil rights leaders across the south vowed to fight on with the campaign to have the death penalty abolished. Richard Dieter, director of the Death Penalty Information Centre, said it was a clear wake-up call to politicians across the US.

"They weren't expecting such passion from people in opposition to the death penalty," he said. "There's a widely held perception that all Americans are united in favour of executions, but this message came across loud and clear that many people are not happy with it."

Brian Evans of Amnesty, which led the campaign to spare Davis's life, said that there was a groundswell in America of people "who are tired of a justice system that is inhumane and inflexible and allows executions where there is clear doubt about guilt". He predicted the debate would now be conducted with renewed energy.

Martina Correia, Davis's sister, who kept vigil at the prison until the end, said that a movement had been formed that would transcend her brother's death. Sitting in a wheelchair as she battles cancer, she said: "If you can get millions of people to stand up against this, we can end the death penalty."

But so far national politicians have refrained from entering the debate. White House press secretary Jay Carney said: "It is not appropriate for the president of the United States to weigh in on specific cases like this one, which is a state prosecution."

Rick Perry, the leading contender for the Republican nomination and a strong supporter of the death penalty, has made no public statement on the Davis case. His presence in the Republican race guarantees that the issue of capital punishment will remain in the spotlight in a way it hasn't for years.

Davis was executed for the 1989 murder of Mark MacPhail, who was working off duty as a security guard when he intervened to help a homeless person being attacked. Davis was implicated by another man, Sylvester Coles. But key witnesses have come forward to say their evidence was wrong, and others have testified under oath that Coles was the killer.

Raphael Warnock, pastor of the Ebenezer Baptist church in Atlanta, where Martin Luther King had his ministry, said: "Through this, America is being transformed. This is one of those watershed moments when a human evil and injustice that is part of the norm suddenly becomes questioned and challenged."

The Guardian Weekly 30.09.11

Capital punishment

Dying out

Little by little, countries are ditching[1] the death penalty

ON SEPTEMBER 19th Abdul Hamid al-Fakki, a Sudanese, was executed in Saudi Arabia for the crime of "sorcery". On September 21st Troy Davis, a black man convicted of shooting an off-duty white policeman, was executed in the American state of Georgia. Protests that the evidence against him was flawed proved fruitless.

Despite these cases the death penalty, on the statute books since the days of Hammurabi, is disappearing in much of the world. More than two-thirds of countries have done away with it either in law or in practice. The latest is Benin. In August the west African country committed itself to abolishing capital punishment permanently. The number of countries that carry out judicial killings fell from 41 in 1995 to 23 in 2010, according to Amnesty International, a pressure group. China (chiefly), Iran, North Korea, and Yemen accounted for most of the executions. Votes against the death penalty at the UN General Assembly have passed with big and growing majorities since 2007. Capital punishment has virtually gone in Europe (only Belarus still uses it, most recently in July). This year China whittled down[2] its list of crimes punishable by death.

Yet for all the apparent momentum, capital punishment remains entrenched in the Middle East and north Africa, and in parts of Asia, notably China. Jacqueline Macalesher of Penal Reform International, a lobby group, thinks the Arab spring could be a new spur to abolition, though she worries that executing political enemies may prove attractive in the short run.

The other big exception is America, where two-thirds of states still have the death penalty. A leading Republican candidate for the presidency, Rick Perry, is governor of Texas, the state that uses it most. The state has carried out a record 236 executions in his nearly 11 years as governor. Mr Perry says he loses no sleep over it, and many voters feel the same.

But the abolitionist trend seems inexorable. In March Illinois became the fourth state in four years to scrap[3] the death penalty. Maryland, Connecticut and California may follow suit. Squeezed state budgets are eroding enthusiasm. The cost of fighting protracted legal battles and maintaining separate facilities for those condemned to death looks increasingly unaffordable when schools and libraries are being closed. California alone has more than 700 people on death row.

Bryan Stevenson, founder of the Equal Justice Initiative, a pressure group that espouses abolition, ascribes increasing unhappiness over the death penalty to a long-term growth in sensitivity to human rights. A growing number mind that the death penalty in America falls disproportionately on blacks and poor people. The chance that innocent folk may be executed counts for more, with many, than the deterrent effect of capital punishment (itself questioned by academic studies). Gruesome details about the mechanics of executions also stoke public disquiet.

Pressure to get into international clubs has also propelled abolition. The Council of Europe, a Strasbourg-based talking shop that requires members to accede to the European Convention on Human Rights, has made the death penalty a bar to membership. That (plus other things such as election rigging) has left Belarus's application with rigor mortis.

The Economist September 24th 2011

[1] to ditch: to get rid of; *here*: to abolish
[2] to whittle down: to reduce
[3] to scrap: to get rid of; *here*: to abolish

A cartoon by Clay Bennett, published in the *Chattanooga Times Free Press*, September 21, 2011

Two Gallup poll charts on opinions in the United States

October 13, 2011

Are you in favor of the death penalty for a person convicted of murder?

1936-2011 trend

- - - - % In favor ——— % Opposed

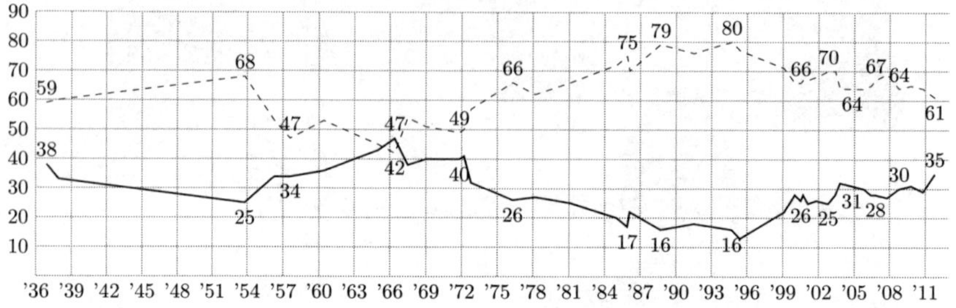

November 8, 2010

If you could choose between the following two approaches, which do you think is the better penalty for murder?

- - - - % The death penalty ——— % Life imprisonment, with absolutely no possibility of parole

·········· % No opinion

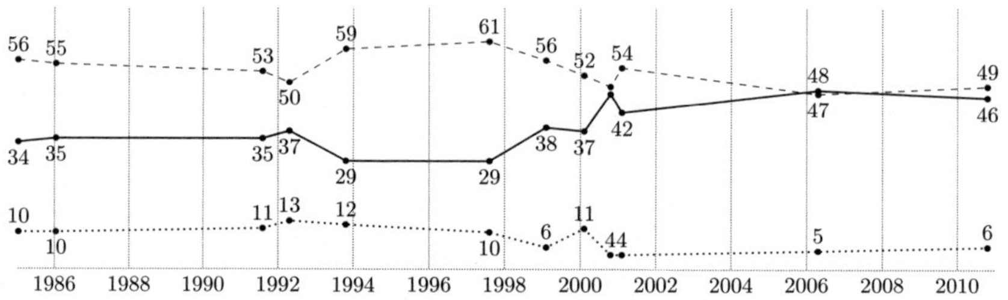

2. Steady

a. Tableau de synthèse

Cf. page suivante.

b. Theme: the death penalty

- **Question:** To what extent is the death penalty still supported and carried out worldwide and more particularly in the US?
- **Outline:**
  I. A legal means despite pressure against
  II. A political issue
  III. Morals and ethics: people's reactions

Or:

  I. Inequity/points of view
  II. In spite of global fall, the case of the US
  III. Abolition is gaining ground

3. Go

The death penalty at the bar

Capital punishment again hit the headlines in September 2011 with the execution of a black man, Troy Davis, in Georgia, USA, rekindling the debate about that form of justice: to what extent is the death penalty still supported and enforced worldwide and more particularly in America? That is the issue raised by a biased *Guardian* article and a cartoon focusing on the iniquity of Davis's case, an *Economist* article assessing the overall global decline of such a sentence and two polls about Americans' opinions. What can be said about this legal means? How does the political sphere react to it? And people?

Execution fuels row… *The Guardian*, Sept. 2011	Dying out *The Economist*, Sept. 2011	Cartoon, Clay Bennett *Chattanooga Times Free Press*, Sept. 2011	Two Gallup poll charts on opinions in the US Oct. 2011 & Nov. 2010
Basis: Troy Davis's execution → debate revived over death penalty Article against death penalty	Basis: Troy Davis's execution Worldwide death penalty decline but a last few "strongholds"	Basis: Troy Davis's case	Pro death penalty > opponents for murderers though pro-death penalty almost = pro-life imprisonment if choice Few people are indifferent
Davis's story: 1989 accused of murder; 1991 conviction; since then witness have recanted + further clearing evidence; Sept2011 execution by lethal injection Location: Atlanta, Georgia, MLK's home → historical place & moment			
Reactions: Against: Protests in Georgia & Washington & abroad, esp. relatives (Davis's sister) & civil rights groups Conviction anti-death penalty movement increasing because "inhumane, inflexible" & possibly unfair Silence: Contrarily, no politicians' reaction – neither the president nor traditional death penalty advocates such as Rick Perry who's running for Republican candidacy	Movement against death penalty: Benin, last country to abolish it UN motions China lists fewer death penalty-related crimes The Arab Spring might foster further abolitions In the US, Illinois abolished it – 4th state in 4 years. Maybe Maryland, Connecticut and California soon Reasons: diplomatic & international pressure (ban to EU membership); growing human right awareness; expensive sentence in budget cut context; biased sentencing; no deterring effect; disgusting method, error margin	Justice is blind & upside-down indifference iniquity → against death penalty	
	Execution in Saudi Arabia for sorcery Execution of T. Davis in US despite fuzzy proofs But global decline overall		
	Death penalty in less than 1/3 countries (41→21, 1995 → 2010) China > Iran, North Korea, the Arab world, the US (2/3 states esp. Texas & its Rep. would-be candidate), only Belarus in Europe, part of Asia For whom: getting rid of political enemies, "sorcerers", murderers		

The death penalty is still legal in less than one third of countries, with China ranking first, followed by Iran, North Korea, Yemen, Middle Eastern and North African countries, Belarus in Europe, plus two-thirds of American states (for instance Texas and Georgia). It is mainly used for those convicted of murder (such as Davis) but *the Economist* reports also a case of "sorcery" in Saudi Arabia and mentions a now-reduced Chinese list of offences punishable by death as well as political enemies.

Though legal, there could be strong economic and diplomatic pressure to entice those countries and states to abandon it. Indeed it is argued that such long-lasting procedures are costly and hardly affordable for a state in dire straits. Moreover, international governmental and non-governmental organisations such as the United Nations and the Council of Europe are getting increasingly adamant against capital punishment. For instance Belarus cannot join the EU.

As to politicians, they seem to be divided. For instance, there is the case of the Arab world whose revolutions could either boost executions so as to get rid of political enemies or lead onto the path of abolition, according to a lobbyist in *The Economist*. Besides more and more countries – such as Benin recently – and US states – such as Illinois and possibly soon Maryland, Connecticut and California – are doing away with the death penalty. Nonetheless some forefront leaders as Rick Perry, the Republican governor of Texas, running for the presidency in 2012, though definitely a strong supporter – his state carrying out a record number of executions – did not comment on Davis's thorny case; neither did President Obama – reportedly distinguishing federal and state affairs.

But people did react and abolition is seemingly gaining ground. Figures, for instance, point out that though Americans still favour capital punishment for murderers (about 60%), even over life imprisonment (49% against 46%), the gap is narrow and the support getting weaker.

Troy Davis was an epitomy for abolitionists. Indeed, accused of killing a white policeman in 1989 and sentenced to death in 1991, despite a lack of convincing evidence and flawed testimonies, he was eventually executed. That triggered a wave of protests both at home, nationwide and worldwide with both his relatives and humanitarian groups siding against the unfairness of his case. They argued that justice was blinded, racist, non-deterring, inhumane and unfair, a portrait that is quite vividly drawn by C. Bennet with his cartoon although it may also denounce the indifference of lawyers and citizens. More generally, the death penalty is said to be against human rights.

So, on the wane, but not defunct yet.

540 words

File 8

Tuition fees

e3a 2012

I. Ready

CONCOURS ARTS ET MÉTIERS ParisTech - ESTP- ARCHIMEDE

Épreuve de Langue Vivante MP - PC - PSI

Durée 3 h

Si, au cours de l'épreuve, un candidat repère ce qui lui semble être une erreur d'énoncé, d'une part il le signale au chef de salle, d'autre part il le signale sur sa copie et poursuit sa composition en indiquant les raisons des initiatives qu'il est amené à prendre.

Pour cette épreuve, l'usage des machines (calculatrices, traductrices,...) et de dictionnaires est interdit.

Vous rédigerez dans la langue choisie et en 400 mots une synthèse des documents proposés. Vous indiquerez avec précision à la fin de votre synthèse le nombre de mots qu'elle comporte. Un écart de 10% en plus ou en moins sera accepté. Votre synthèse comportera un titre comptabilisé dans le nombre de mots.

Le candidat a obligation de traiter le sujet dans la langue qu'il a choisie au moment de son inscription au concours.

Tournez la page S.V.P.

ANGLAIS

Vous rédigerez en anglais et en 400 mots une synthèse des documents proposés. Vous indiquerez avec précision à la fin de votre synthèse le nombre de mots qu'elle comporte. Un écart de 10% en plus ou en moins sera accepté. Votre synthèse comportera un titre comptabilisé dans le nombre de mots.

DOCUMENT 1

University admissions could create two-tier system, committee warns

Government plans to transform the way universities recruit students risk creating a two-tier system that could hit social mobility, a committee of MPs warns [...]. Currently, English universities have a fixed yearly allocation of student places, but the coalition proposes to let institutions take on unlimited numbers of the best-performing students. But the government has also announced that 20,000 places will be set aside for universities charging fees of £7,500 or less. The business, innovation and skills select committee warns that the proposals will channel more students – particularly those with low grades – into "a low-cost model of higher education." The higher education sector could be polarised into "traditional" universities versus a "low-cost" alternative. "This could have undesirable consequences for social mobility if able candidates from lower socio-economic backgrounds felt constrained to choose lower-cost provision," the MPs say. "Further education colleges (and other providers) are capable of offering excellent low-cost and high-quality provision, but they may not offer the same experience as a student might receive in a traditional university."

The report urges ministers to monitor the social mix at universities and take swift action if a two-tier sector emerges. The select committee's inquiry heard evidence that "mid-ranking" universities faced the greatest difficulties because they are likely to lose high-performing students to more prestigious institutions and cannot bid for extra places under the £7,500 margin.

In response to the proposals, 24 universities and three further education (FE) colleges have applied to lower fees to an average of £7,500 or less, the Office for Fair Access [OFFA] says. The MPs call for a "student premium" like the pupil premium for schools. Nick Clegg, the deputy prime minister, announced a student premium last October. It became a national scholarship scheme aimed at 50,000 students a year, which will provide a package which may include "fee waivers", discounted accommodation or cash.

The MPs' report says that financial support should be focused on providing money for living costs rather than fee waivers which reduce a student's future debt. The MPs said the government had faced difficulties in communicating the changes, and should have handled this better.

"A key aspect of the debate on the increase in tuition fees was disagreements over how much a student would expect to be charged for a university course," the MPs noted. The committee concluded that most new undergraduates next year will be charged a tuition fee of £9,000. Figures published by the OFFA, which vets proposals to widen the social mix at universities, show the average fee across the sector will be £8,393 next year. However, the MPs say that the use of this average is "less helpful and relevant" to students than the most commonly charged fee.

The report urges the government to use the latter figure when publicising the reforms. [...] A wide range of factors affect how likely it is that student loans will be repaid, including the initial size of loans, the proportion of men and women – as male graduates tend to earn more than female graduates – and the future performance of the economy, the MPs said. "Regardless of the arguments both for and against a higher level of student contribution, the financial sustainability of the new system is untested. As a result, an unprecedented level of uncertainty has been introduced into higher education finances with success dependent on a large number of variables over which the government has little control." Adrian Bailey MP, chair of the committee said: "The government's reforms of higher education are wide-ranging and comprehensive. While we welcome the aim to put students at the heart of the system, that ambition will only be realised if the government delivers the reforms on time and as a package."

"The start of the new academic year is less than a year away and many key aspects of the reforms – including vital support for students – are currently out for consultation. The government will have to work overtime to deliver these reforms so that next years' intake of students have the information and support they were promised in exchange for their increased contributions to their education."

Jeevan Vasagar,
The Guardian, November 2011

DOCUMENT 2

Families may "move from England to avoid tuition fee rise"

The rising cost of a university degree in England could create "fee refugees" as parents move to Scotland and Wales to escape huge debts.

An analysis by the Government's Higher Education Funding Council for England [HEFCE] said families may flee over the border to avoid fees of up to £9,000 in 2012. Parents living "close to the borders" are among those most likely to relocate to another country, it was claimed [...].

A move from England to Scotland could save students as much as £36,000 for a four year degree because of sharp differences in fees policies operated by devolved governments across the UK. The comments came as it emerged that the Scottish Executive could carry out checks on applicants to ensure they are legitimate residents and not attempting to exploit the generous funding system north of the border. From next year, English students will be forced to pay up to £9,000 wherever they study but Scottish undergraduates will be given free tuition. Fees for Welsh students will be fixed at £3,465 and those in Northern Ireland will pay a similar amount, but only if they stay in their own region.

The system has already caused outrage in England, with several students pursuing legal action against the Scottish government amid claims that the fee rises will breach their human rights. The Scottish Conservatives have branded the plans "vindictive" and warned that it would "stir up resentment in the rest of the UK against Scotland". A paper presented to a HEFCE board meeting warns that there "may be issues with families, particularly those close to the borders, seeking to domicile themselves in Wales or Scotland in order to benefit from favourable fee arrangements." The report adds: "This could have distortive effects on local economies and housing markets if it occurred with significant numbers."

Bob Osborne, emeritus professor of public policy at Ulster University, told *Times Higher Education* magazine that if a family "was living 15 miles from the Scottish border then you can see how they might try to wangle it." But he doubted there was going to be a "mass exodus of people from Surrey to Glasgow." The Scottish Executive has already said children whose parents move to Scotland for their careers will be eligible for a free university education. But families who seek to exploit the system by buying a home north of the Border will not. A spokesman said the Student Awards Agency for Scotland will decide on a case-by-case basis, with people not living north of the border for long likely to be scrutinised.

The HEFCE paper also warned that there is a "question of affordability" attached to the reforms for devolved administrations. Most countries are committed to subsidising students' tuition even if they study outside their home country and budgets may be stretched if universities in England put up their tuition fees, it was claimed.

Graeme Paton,
The Daily Telegraph, November 2011

DOCUMENT 3

University fees do not deter school leavers

School leavers have not been deterred from applying to university by the introduction of higher tuition fees this year, although older students do appear to have been put off by the extra costs, interim figures from the University and College Admissions Service [UCAS] suggest.

From October, English universities will be able to charge up to £9,000 a year to undergraduates from the UK and European Union, up from £3,375. The rise has sparked widespread concern that poor students in particular will be discouraged from applying.

The number of British 18-year-olds who have applied to university for 2012 so far is 2.4 per cent lower than last year, the UCAS figures show. According to official population projections, this fall is broadly in line with a demographic decline in the number of people in that age bracket.

However, the interim UCAS figures account for the number of applications received by mid-December and may improve by January 15, the deadline for most courses. Mary Curnock Cook, UCAS chief executive, said: "Evidence of a late surge [...] is now emerging."

"Applicants are taking longer to research their choices but the applications flow has speeded up, as these statistics show. It remains too early to make predictions about the final year on year figures but we will be able to get a clearer picture after the deadline has passed."

Previous increases in fees did not have a sustained impact on application rates, with would-be students continuing to apply in rising numbers.

The decision to raise fees was a stern test of coalition unity: in opposition, the Liberal Democrats had pledged to oppose any fee increases. Demonstrations against the fee rises culminated in an attack by angry protesters on the Conservative party's headquarters in Westminster.

While the rate for younger students appears to be holding steady, the number of older applicants from the UK and abroad fell 13 per cent. This decline reduced the total volume of applications by 6.4 per cent. The number of non-EU applicants, who are not affected directly by the fee cap changes, is up 13.3 per cent.

Looking only at larger subject groups, the largest declines in applications were for the social sciences and social studies, which registered a 12 per cent fall. Applications for medicine, medical and veterinary sciences and the physical sciences were broadly flat.

Les Ebdon, chair of the Million+ universities think-tank and vice-chancellor of Bedfordshire University, said: "Ministers need to launch a campaign to ensure that older students understand the [student] loan system and the opportunities available."

He added: "A failure to do so will overshadow the success the government has had in persuading younger applicants that university remains one of the best career moves that they can make."

Chris Cook,
The Financial Times, January 2012

Tournez la page S.V.P.

2. Steady

a. Tableau de synthèse

Cf. page suivante.

b. Theme: rise in tuition fees in England

- **Question:** What are the reactions to and possible consequences of the rise in tuition fees in England?
- **Outline:**
  1. political/governmental view
  2. students and families
  3. universities

Or:

  1. facts
  2. risks and reactions
  3. recommendations to the government

"University admissions could create a two-tier system." *The Guardian*, Nov. 2011	"Families may 'move from England'..." *The Daily Telegraph*, Nov. 2011	"Universities fees do not deter school leavers" *The Financial Times*, Jan2012
Warnings from an MP business, innovation and skills select committee about the government plans to increase tuition fees and changing recruitment rules – risk of a two-tier unfair system in England	Due to the increase in tuition fees in England, some families may be tempted to move to Wales or Scotland where tuition are lower or free, a challenge for the education authorities there An HEFCE paper – Higher Education Funding Council for England	UCAS assessing university applications after a tuition fees increase has been announced – contrast between school leavers and older students but interim figures, nothing definite yet; dealing mid-January
<u>Facts</u>: newly unlimited places for best students; 20,000 places for less expensive universities (£7,500 & below as another 24 institutions have offered); student premium, i.e. national scholarship scheme (living costs or fees reductions); most new undergraduates will be charged about £9,000, i.e. more student contribution to higher education finances <u>Risks/blames:</u> two-tier system, i.e. traditional vs low-cost universities; social mobility jeopardised; lower social mix at universities; bad communications from the government; financial sustainability of the scheme is doubtful as so many factors have to be taken into account → higher education finances could be right <u>Recommendations</u>: take action if social mix reduced; give money for living costs rather than fees cuts; the most usual fees figures should be used; the reforms have to be delivered on time and clearly <u>Actors</u>: government, MP committee, Office for fair Access (OFFA), universities & students	<u>Facts</u>: fees increased up to £9,000 in England; free fees in Scotland; fees at £3,465 in Wales & Northern Ireland <u>Risks/Consequences</u>: people, esp. those near the border moving to Wales and Scotland, possibly exploiting the system; anger against Scotland from the rest of the UK; bad effects on local economies & housing markets if a lot but a moot point; stretched budgets for countries subsidising expat students <u>Reaction</u>: students' outrage because against their human rights; a case-by-case basis for litigious cases	<u>Facts</u>: fees increased up to £9,000 in England; so far school leavers not deterred though fewer but in keeping with demography but older students yes; more applications in the run-up; previous increases had no impact on application figures; more non-EU applicants; variations according to subjects; the Lib-Dem had pledged not to increase fees <u>Concerns</u>: poor students may be deterred <u>Reactions</u>: demos in London <u>Recommendations</u>: launching a campaign to be understood well otherwise success of the reform jeopardised

3. Go

Rising tuition fees in England

The British coalition government's decision to increase tuition fees in England – despite Lib-Dem previous pledges not to do so – raised a heated debate. What are the reactions to, and possible consequences of, this decision? Three articles – from *the Guardian, the Daily Telegraph and The Financial Times* – published in late 2011-early 2012 analyse the facts and risks entailed and recommend a few measures to the government.

English universities can increase their fees up to £9, 000 starting in 2012 so that students will thus contribute more to higher education finances. Most new undergraduates will be charged that amount but there will be unlimited places for the best students plus 20, 000 places at less expensive universities (24 such institutions have offered to charge £7, 500 or less, the Office for Fair Access says) and a national scholarship scheme (for living costs or fees cuts). *The Telegraph* stresses the contrast with the rest of the UK, Scotland having no tuition fees and Wales and Northern Ireland charging far less than England so that families might be tempted to cross borders. Yet *The Financial Times* notes that according to the agency in charge of admissions (UCAS) past fees increases had had no impact, and they have not observed any note-worthy fall in applications for 2012 despite a few understandable variations.

Students, however, demonstrated against the rise and some were outraged by the Scottish government's will to ensure applicants are really living in Scotland – on a case-by-case basis for litigious cases. More broadly, an MP select committee warned against the risk of an unfair two-tier system in England pitting traditional expensive universities against low-cost ones. People worry that poor students may be deterred. Social mobility might be consequently jeopardised and students might end up coming from similar walks of life. People also expressed doubts over the financial sustainability of the scheme since many elements have to be factored in. Another official paper underlined the risk for English families close to Scotland or Wales to move there and possibly exploit the system, which would be detrimental to local economies and housing markets – albeit a moot point. Besides the budgets of countries subsidising their students abroad might be stretched – still there are more non-EU applicants this year.

While *The Financial Times* reports the launch of a public relation campaign being recommended to ensure the government's reform is well understood, the MP committee advises to take action in case of a lower social mix at universities, to give priority to living costs in scholarships, to use the most relevant figures and to deliver reforms on time and clearly.

Results are expected.

439 words

Table des matières

Préface **3**

Partie I. Méthode 5

Chapitre 1 : L'épreuve de synthèse **7**
1. Centrale 9
2. e3a 10

Chapitre 2 : Aborder les différents types de document **11**
1. Un article de presse 13
2. Un dessin humoristique 16
3. Un graphique, un tableau 19
4. Un extrait littéraire 23
5. Une publicité 25
6. Une photographie 28

Chapitre 3 : Comment procéder **35**
1. Méthode et gestion du temps 37
2. Phraséologie 38
3. Exercices 49

Chapitre 4 : Les critères **57**
1. Richesse et correction grammaticale 59
2. Étendue et précision lexicale 61
3. Restitution des informations nécessaires 65
4. Structuration, confrontation des documents et enchaînement ordonné 65
5. Titre, problématisation introductive et sources 68

Partie II. Entraînements et sujets d'annales **69**

File 1 : Plastics 71
File 2 : The special relationship 83
File 3 : Space debris 95
File 4 : Health 107
File 5 : Technologies & privacy 119
File 6 : 9/11 – Centrale 2012 (MP, PC, PSI) 129
File 7 : The death penalty – Centrale 2012 (TSI) 139
File 8 : Tuition fees – e3a 2012 149

Achevé d'imprimer en février 2013 par Normandie Roto Impression s.a.s., 61250 Lonrai
N° d'impression : 130717 – Dépôt légal : mars 2013 – *Imprimé en France*